Memories of Childhood

Martin Nicholson

ISBN 978-1-4709-6042-1

2nd Edition

Author's note

Memories of Childhood was first published privately in 2008, mainly for family and friends. I am now re-issuing it as the first part of what I hope will be four volumes of memoirs up to my retirement from the Diplomatic Service in 1997. The manuscript is the same as in the first edition, aside from a couple of factual corrections.

Among many debts of gratitude, I owe one in particular to my son Colin, who has not only tirelessly pushed at the boundaries of my memory, but has also taught me some of the basics of editing.

Martin Nicholson

Twickenham

March 2011

In memory of my parents,

who gave me my childhood,

and to my siblings, with whom

I was privileged to share it

CONTENTS

One

'White for a Brazilian'

My Brazilian birth certificate is precise. It states that I was born 'Martin Buchanan Nicholson' at the *Hospital dos Estrangeiros* in Rio de Janeiro at ten past four in the afternoon of 12th August 1937, male, white-skinned, the legitimate son of Carroll Parker Nicholson and Nancy Esther Nicholson. The exhaustive certificate also names my grandparents – on the paternal side Colin and Winifred Nicholson and on the maternal side Clive and Eleanor Levi.

I remember the Strangers' Hospital, as we always mistranslated it. Not, of course, from the day of my birth, but from eight years later when, back in Rio, we would pass it on the *Leme Bonde*, the tram that took us to the beach at Copacabana. Every time we went by my mother would say: 'That is the hospital where you were born'. On one occasion we saw two little boys scrambling up the slope to the hospital: 'Mummy,' I asked, 'are those boys going to the hospital to be born?'

My Brazilian birth certificate meant that the local authorities considered me Brazilian, which caused a few problems later on. And not only the authorities – our jet black maid Victalina was puzzled when she first saw me: 'He's very white for a Brazilian!' she mused. My parents were in fact very English. My father, a mechanical engineer by profession, worked for Shell and had been induced to go to Rio by the promise that his salary would be doubled. With my elder brother Robin, born three years to the day before me, they set sail from Tilbury Docks on the Thames estuary on 1st February 1936. They were accompanied by Adele Haes, my mother's Australian third cousin, known to all as 'Top' or 'Toppy' because she was small but had a disproportionately thick head of hair which was fuzzy and stuck out a lot. She had come over from Australia to see Britain and had helped to look after Robin in England. She was to be with us on and off throughout my childhood, helping out with the growing family.

The party arrived in Rio on 17th February, in the middle of carnival. It was not the easiest moment to start a foreign posting. Suffering from the heat, they were holed up in a hotel room while singing and dancing continued night and day outside. As she wrote later, my mother thought the world had gone mad. Anxious to get out of the centre, they quickly found a small, uncomfortably furnished house, *Rua Joanna Angelica 30*, near the beach in Ipanema. Even so, life was difficult. Inflation (unknown in England at the time) ate into my father's increased salary. My mother found herself shopping in the markets for the cheapest goods without knowledge of the local customs or language. She had to dismiss three maids, who had run rings round her, before she found the loyal Victalina. In addition her mother Nellie Levi made the long journey from Sutton Coldfield, near Birmingham, to assist at the birth of her second grandchild.

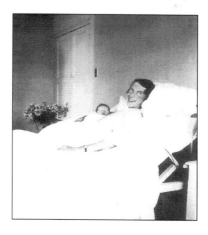

In Mum's arms: 48 hours old, in the
Strangers' Hospital, Rio de Janeiro

In Toppy's arms: with Mum, Dad and Robin in
our Prudente de Moraes house, Rio, 1938

From the wry remarks Mum would make later in life I gathered that Grannie Nellie needed quite as much assistance herself in adjusting to the unfamiliar and uncomfortable surroundings of Rio.

I was nearly called Patrick. Martin was altogether a more suitable name, being the one my immigrant Great Great Grandfather Meyer Wertheimer had adopted when he was naturalised and which had then trickled down through the generations. 'We all like the name MARTIN better than Patrick,' wrote my grandfather Clive Levi approvingly to his daughter the day after my birth. My second name, Buchanan, was Nellie Levi's maiden name (she being the first in my mother's family to be of non-Jewish descent) and was distributed to all of us children to keep it in the family. I was christened on 16th September 1937 in the Anglican Christ Church in Rio by the Rev A.W.Crudgington — 'the almost Reverend', my

In Victalina's arms:
With Robin, Rio

father liked to call him, as he was wearing a short cassock made for the tropics. He must have done a thorough job at the font, for it provoked Robin to ask, 'Mummy, what for that man washing Martin's hair?'

I had two godparents in attendance, Bobby Hinrichsen, the doctor who attended my birth, and Ottilie Sherring, the wife of a former Shell colleague of my father. We lost touch with Bobby Hinrichsen fairly quickly, but Ottilie and Ian Sherring welcomed me on an adventurous trip to their country farm during our second stay in Rio. I had two more godparents in England – Priscilla Ragg (later Thomson) from Four Oaks in Sutton Coldfield, who had been my mother's bridesmaid, and my father's Cambridge friend Dick Burrough, a lawyer and cricketer.

In September 1937 we moved to *Rua Prudente de Moraes*

128, still in Ipanema. As it was not far away the movers shuttled our things from one house to the other. Only the newest acquisition was left behind in the turmoil. That was me, but I was soon discovered gurgling in my pram in the garden, blissfully unaware that I had been abandoned. It was in the new house that I celebrated my first birthday, which was of course also Robin's fourth. My mother described it in meticulous detail in a letter to her mother. It was a lavish occasion, two months in preparation, which started in the morning with a small celebration at Robin's nursery school, and continued with a tea party: six guests, many presents and two cakes. I wept when my one candle was blown out.

We were back in England on leave for my second birthday. We had arrived in early April 1939 and stayed with my mother's parents at their home, 'Camberley', 5 Beaconsfield Road, Sutton Coldfield. There I started my gardening under the tuition of my grandfather. We have some idyllic photos of the stay, among them a 'four generations' photograph (see page 17) showing my great grandmother Julia Levi (born Wertheimer), her son Clive, his daughter Nancy and her children, Robin and me. I find that photo a source of wonder, linking me as it does with an ancestor born in 1855. It is also very poignant: my mother was never again to see her father, who died of stomach cancer a couple of months later, or her grandmother, who died in 1944 while we were still abroad. With war looming as well it was an anxious time.

My father returned to South America first – not to Rio but to

Buenos Aires, capital of Argentina, on a new posting, arriving on the Royal Mail Liner *Highland Patriot* on 19th August 1939. For the first time, but by no means the last, he was separated from his family by the Atlantic Ocean. He immediately set to work to find a house for us while we waited for my mother to have an abdominal operation and for her father to have an operation for his cancer. Then on 3rd September Britain declared war on Germany. My father immediately registered for military service with the British Consulate in Buenos Aires. Had he been accepted we would not of course have sailed out to join him. He had no wish to fight but was intensely patriotic and was determined that if he was enlisted it should be as a volunteer and not a conscript. In the event he was told that because of his engineering qualifications Shell required him to remain in his current employment. But he learnt this only on 7th September, two days before Mum, Robin and I (still in England) were due to sail, and he didn't know whether we had got the

In carnival mood: Rio, February 1939

information. 'Still no cable from London about Nancy,' he wrote to his mother on the same day, 'I wish I knew what was happening.' The cables must have got through in the end, for we set sail on Sunday, 10th September – late, as our ship, the *Patriot's* sister ship *Highland Princess*, had first to be painted in its wartime livery of grey and fitted with a gun. We learnt of the delay only after setting off from Sutton Coldfield, so Shell had to fix us up for a couple of nights at the Euston Hotel in London en route to Tilbury docks. The capital was on high alert – nobody knew of course that this was only the start of the 'phoney war'. A black out was being strictly enforced. Most children had already been evacuated, and Robin and I attracted curious and disapproving looks. To escape the heat and tedium of the hotel my mother took us to my father's aunt Ruth Parrott in Clapham for the day: 'She has a good Air Raid Shelter so I think we are as well off with her as anywhere,' my mother wrote to her parents from the hotel on 7th September.

The voyage too was governed by wartime precautions. We travelled under escort to Lisbon, and then zigzagged across the ocean to avoid submarines, with male passengers drafted into submarine lookout duties. We made our next landfall a good twenty one days later – in Rio, which a few months previously had been our home and where we were able to see friends. The ship was uncomfortable: it was blacked out at night and the lounges became stiflingly hot. I was very spoilt and enjoyed it. We had Toppy with us, so my mother was not over-burdened with looking after us, but the tedium told: 'I have played quite a lot of bridge between tea & dinner,' she wrote to her mother, 'it shows to what depths of boredom I have arrived.' Her letter is written on ship's paper, but without the name of the ship, and is undated. Passengers had been instructed to leave as few clues as possible as to the whereabouts of a British ship in mid-Atlantic in case the Germans intercepted the mail.

Four generations: my great grandmother Julia Levi (84),
my grandfather Clive Levi (65), my mother Nancy Nicholson (32),
my brother Robin (5) and me (2), Sutton Coldfield, August 1939

We were overjoyed to find my father waiting when we docked at the Uruguayan capital of Montevideo, and he sailed with us for the last night of the journey before we arrived in Buenos Aires on 5th October 1939 after 26 days at sea. He took us to a boarding house in the suburb of Temperley, where a new chapter in my life began – we were to spend nearly six years in Argentina followed by a brief return to Brazil.

Two

South America:

Wartime Abundance

Temperley was on the railway line leading south from Buenos Aires: its official postal address ended with 'FCS' – *Ferrocarril del Sud* (Southern Railway). The town had grown out of the station, built in 1871 by the British entrepreneur George Temperley, and a good half of its population was English-speaking. It seems appropriate that our first home was the boarding house on the square outside the station. It was also ideal for Robin, who was mad on trains.

We stayed there a good month or more while the house we were to rent for the duration of our stay in Argentina was made ready – the previous tenant, Mrs Atkins, had to move out, our furniture had to arrive from Brazil, and some decorating had to be done. While we were waiting my mother suffered the bereavement she knew was coming – the death of her father on 25th October 1939. As she wrote to her mother, she felt helpless being so far away, remorseful that she had not been able to show her father the appreciation she felt for him, but thankful that we had been with them during our leave.

Our new home, which has since been demolished and replaced by flats, was called Blink Bonnie and was located at *Avenida Fernandez trescientos treinta y uno*. I spell out the number, 331, as it was one of the first I learnt by heart in Spanish, as was our telephone number – *Temperley dos-seis-dos-dos*. My father had found the house on 28th August, while the rest of the family were still in England. He looked at half a dozen houses that day – carefully pasting the advertisements from the *Buenos Aires Herald* into a notebook – and by the side of the Blink Bonnie advert he had written GOOD SIZE, CASTLE STYLE! NICE. It was large and airy, and complemented by a big garden with stables and a chicken run. The castle style that my father referred to was created by distinctive battlements topping off the front walls. This was to be my

Blink Bonnie: our house in Temperley

world for the next five and a half years, and it is here that my own memories of childhood really begin.

We boys were given the grand front room, really the dining room, as our playroom. Our landlady Mrs Lauder could never understand that. We ate in a smaller room on the other side of the hall. From there we could see the front gate, wag our fingers at beggars and hawkers, and jump with excitement when my father walked through the gate at lunchtime on Saturday.

In the playroom, we kept our toys in a large built-in dresser, Robin's side tidy, mine less so. Minibrix (the forerunner of Lego, but with rubber rather than plastic bricks) and Meccano (a metal construction kit) were the staple, but we each gradually built up our collection of Dinky Toys (die-cast miniature model cars) as well. When Robin later went off to boarding school, his last remark to me – very sweetly – would be, 'You can play with any of my toys.' This became one of our family sayings. The pride of our playroom was Robin's '0' gauge model railway, which grew slowly but confidently into a permanent network with stations, viaducts, engine sheds and other architecture designed and built in wood by my father in his workshop – the old stables towards the bottom of the garden.

Robin and I were very good, really. The naughtiest thing we did in the house was to play with streamers on the stairs when my mother was out for the day. The staircase doubled back on itself and could be viewed through the open banisters on the landing. We would let the streamers down from the landing and haul them up again – an innocent enough pastime, but one which was forbidden, probably because our safety-conscious parents didn't like the thought of us playing around on the stairs. Anecdotes passed on in letters by my parents to their parents show me developing the ability to talk my way out of trouble: 'I did it when I wasn't looking' became a family favourite.

Although Toppy had come out with us from England, she had gone home to Australia soon after, so on these occasions I suppose we were in the charge of our maid, María Griffiths – not a trace of Welsh left in her, despite the name. At the end of 1940 she was joined by her fourteen year old sister, Teresa. They had a little room over the kitchen. We got on well with them, without speaking their language (at least I didn't). One day my mother found me sitting on the kitchen table with María in fits of laughter: '*¡Qué gracioso!*' – which means how funny he is, not how gracious.

The garden seemed enormous. To the side of the house was a lawn surrounded by tangerine and lemon trees, which was our cricket field. Behind the house was the patio, where we had our little table and chairs. One job we did there was to de-pip the grapes we plucked off the vine running along a nearby trellis. We picked out the biggest grapes to eat ourselves, but sometimes they would be over-ripe: 'Big one ... too sweet!' Robin would say. Beyond the patio was another lawn, with an enormous palm tree in it. We hung the hammock (a knotted string contraption that followed us all the way back to England) from that tree to another.

Across the lawn and beyond a hedge, the last and most

Carpenters: with Robin and Dad in the old
stable in Blink Bonnie Garden

exciting part of the garden began. To the left was the small chicken run. It was a favourite place of mine. I was once standing at my usual spot, watching the chicks scampering around, when suddenly they appeared at my feet, outside their pen. In a panic I raced towards the house to summon help. I shall never forget the horrible squelch as I trod on one of the little chicks in my flight. By the time my mother and María arrived on the scene, many of the chickens had fallen into the shallow ditch that ran alongside the pen and were drowning. Maria gathered them up and put them in the oven to revive them, but many died. Of course I was the culprit, having evidently allowed the gate to swing open by fiddling with the latch. But I felt no guilt – all my mind would admit to was that at one moment the gate was closed and the chickens safely in their pen, and the next moment the gate had swung open and they were outside. I grumbled at my (rather mild) punishment – to report the incident and my unseemly role in it to our next door neighbours, the Scot-Whytes.

After the chicken pen came a lean-to that served as the laundry room, associated in my mind with brilliant white and deep blue. White because my father would whitewash it every year; deep blue because when Maria washed the sheets she would add a pellet of blue dye, which made them come out sparkling white. Here, too, the several cats which roamed the gardens would give birth to their litters. My father had to drown most of them, otherwise we would have been over-run.

Robin and I had a little hiding place on top of the laundry. There we would sometimes secretly eat peanuts. We would creep unnoticed, or so we thought, right to the front of the garden, climb over the front fence and wait for the peanut seller to come down the road with what looked like a miniature steam engine, where he heated the peanuts. We bought a couple of cones and scooted back to our hiding place. I can't believe we really managed all that away from my mother's eagle eye.

The laundry leaned up against the old stable, which was my father's workshop. An excellent carpenter, he made a wide variety of things – not only bits and pieces for the model railway, but a wheel barrow, a swing, a dining room table and a side-board (the last two still in use today). Robin worked with him, and so did I in a manner of speaking.

Facing the stable was lawn with a couple of fig trees in it. Here I learnt to ride a bicycle. I frequently fell off, as often as not on to an over-ripe fig on the lawn. This made learning to ride a messy business. When the fig concealed a wasp it was painful as well.

On the other side of the lawn my father built a little house out of a large packing case. My mother once found Elaine Scot-Whyte and me sitting motionless on the door-step of this little house, each with a stick in our hand. 'What are you two doing?' she asked. 'Fishing, of course,' we answered dryly. I played a lot with Elaine while Robin was away at boarding school. Her father even built a little step ladder between our two gardens so that we could meet without going out of our respective front gates. But Elaine was a year and a half older than me, and when Robin came back for the holidays she made a bee-line for him. I was wildly jealous.

Beyond the stable was the big chicken run. Here María would chase the fattest hen, take hold of its head and swing it furiously round in the air, a crude but effective way of fulfilling Mrs Beeton's first injunction. Beyond the chicken run was the bonfire site. I once had an accident there. In my little rubber boots I shuffled among the ashes of a spent bonfire, treating it as a sandpit. The boots prevented me from realising the ashes were hot until too late. Another terrified run to my mother, who had to tear off my boots to reveal the blistered feet within.

But life was not all wasp stings and burnt feet. My memories of the sweet corn plantation at the bottom of the garden are entirely pleasant. We called it *chócolo* and would eat it off the cob, lightly boiled, with butter, a special treat. Figs and sweet corn played such a big part in our life that when we settled back in England after the war my parents planted them in the garden of the house they were to spend the rest of their lives in, as well as stringing up the old hammock between two apple trees. The fig trees were still there many years later, though they produced less and less fruit. The sweet corn never produced enough to make it worth while. It was difficult to reproduce Argentine conditions in England.

Feeding the cats: in Blink Bonnie
garden with Robin

Everyday life was punctuated by Christmas and our joint birthday. We had a traditional Christmas tree with real candles which were lit just for a few minutes on Christmas Eve. Like other English children I wrote to Father Christmas. The difference was that Christmas was in the summer, and on Christmas Day we would go to our friends the MacIntyres, who lived down the railway line at Ranelagh, where we had an *asado*, or barbecue, and bathed in their canvas-sided swimming pool. On one occasion Robin had made me a little wooden boat for a Christmas present, which I floated in the pool. On the way back I sat on it in the scramble to get on the train and squashed it flat. I was mortified, but Robin took it all in his stride: for him the fun was always in the making.

Christmas 1940 we spent at home, according to a detailed account my mother sent to England. We had been invited by my father's boss Mr Platt, Shell's General Manager in Argentina, but in the event Robin had swollen neck glands and a temperature and we couldn't go. It was desperately hot, and when we were already in bed on Christmas Eve a spectacular thunderstorm drove a sheet of water across our room. I can still picture that, as I can the colossal aeroplane-shaped hamper that arrived as a Christmas gift from some Shell-Mex contractors with whom my father often worked. After the goodies had been removed, it found a home in our playroom. I was still small enough to be able to sit in it. I persuaded my parents to give me a flying helmet and goggles, and spent many hours in the air, like Snoopy in the Peanuts cartoon.

All I remember of our joint birthday parties is that Robin would have a chocolate cake and I an orange cake. In a letter home reporting our seventh and fourth birthday party in August 1941 my mother describes how she had hoped to buy cakes from the local British community, the proceeds of which went to the War Fund, but the cake makers had shot their bolt catering for sailors from two warships. So at the last minute Mrs Atkins made two sponge cakes for me (split and sandwiched with *dulce de leche*, an Argentine fudge-like delicacy), while my mother made a six-layered chocolate one for Robin. The quantity was necessary, as Robin's entire school had been invited, and sixteen came – in fancy dress. 'Martin looked sweet as a toy rabbit again and Robin was to have been a Teddy Bear but his ears didn't look like a bear but just like a mouse, so I hastily made him a very long tail and he quickly turned into a mouse,' wrote my mother. She was expert at making these costumes out of velvety material and continued to do so for her grandchildren.

The party was only dampened by the unexpected presence of Mrs Platt, who brought her twin sons. The presence of 'the G.M.'s wife' was inhibiting, and the twins, fat, awkward and shy at the best of times, totally lost face when Mrs Harrison, our school teacher, mistook them for girls in their Indian prince costumes.

******

House and garden made a complete world, which I only left when I had to. I had one exotic place of pilgrimage within walking distance, but which I was not allowed to visit on my own – the old car dump. I could stand there for hours looking at the heaps of metal stacked on top of each other. When Robin was taken to the opera (*The Golden Cockerel*) as a special treat, I was allowed to name the thing I would most like to do by way of compensation for being too young for that sort of entertainment. 'The car dump, please,' I requested.

When I was old enough, I started going to Mrs Harrison's school, by horse and cart. The horse was Domingo and the coachman Ramón. The school was a shade old-fashioned – wash your mouth out with soap and water if you are caught telling a lie. I didn't do very well at Mrs Harrison's school. In fact at one point I had to be put down a class. The story in the family is that I spent too much time ogling Elaine Scot-Whyte. My recollection is that I spent more time ogling a girl called Brenda, who wore stockings and showed me where they ended... But the real and more prosaic reason for this slight check in my academic career was, I believe, that I could not find a way of putting the tail on the letter 'n' once I started joined-up writing. I remember having to sit in a classroom on my own, trying to get it right. I would form a hillock on the line and then add the tail, like a hair on a head, knowing that it was wrong, but unable to see how to integrate it into the character. I was very relieved when the mystery was solved – I don't remember how.

I had to do an occasional walk of a couple of blocks with Robin to our piano lesson with Mrs Atkins' daughter Priscilla. We were terrified of being set upon on the way by local boys. We were always on the alert for the 'grey boys' and the 'white boys' – so-called because of the colour of their school smocks. They once invaded the garden to pinch some tangerines, but disappeared pretty quickly when my father came round the corner clutching a mallet. I also remember Robin getting his hand cut by a lone boy who appeared to be holding a broken bottle. We were frightened.

We occasionally visited our landlady, old Mrs Lauder. If she remembered, she would give us some caramel sweets. I'm sure we

Fancy dress: our joint birthday, 1941

were always charming and well-behaved, but inside I had only one thought – will she remember to give us the sweets? We did the occasional grander outing. My mother describes in one of her few surviving letters home how before Christmas 1940 we went into Buenos Aires to spend the money sent us by our grandparents. On these journeys we went by train to Constitución – the Waterloo Station of Buenos Aires. On one such journey I made a famous remark: 'Why are all the stations called *Caballeros* (Gents)?' We also seem to have had a rich social life at the club at Lomas deZamora, one station up the line from Temperley. In another of her letters my mother describes a sports day there, where I showed unexpected concentration to win the potato race. I also won a prize in a flower arranging competition, though in fairness it has to be said that mine was the only entry in my age group. Our social life was completed by visits from Shell friends Jo and 'Hendy' Henderson, and Pita Sheepshanks, whom we got to know through them – friendships which lasted long after we had left South America.

My younger brother Jonathan was born on 30th June 1942, the same day of the month as his late grandfather Clive Levi. This was a dramatic event, which involved a night time dash by taxi to the British Hospital and unwinding the umbilical cord from around poor Jonathan's neck. I can't pretend that for me, approaching five years old, it was a big event. Robin's going off to boarding school at St George's College, Quilmes, also south of Buenos Aires, led to greater changes in my day-to-day life, but I didn't miss him as much as my parents had feared. Indeed, as my father sagely wrote to his mother, 'In many ways it will do [Martin] good as he depended on Robin a lot & Robin's good nature always made him [Robin] do more than his fair share of tidying up.'

We used to go on holiday to Uruguay – just a ferry ride across the River Plate. We stayed at a guest house run by a Scottish lady, Miss Nimmo. It was a bungalow and very open to the natural world outside. To get from room to room you went out on to the veranda. As a result we got a variety of wildlife in our bedroom at night – spiders, lizards and other creepy-crawlies – which made it both exciting and a little frightening. On other holidays in Uruguay we stayed with a Mrs Irving. Robin and I went on one such holiday with a party that didn't include our parents, which made it even more exciting. We played some very grown-up games of pirates with a wrecked ship (probably an old fishing boat) on the beach. In the evenings we played rummy – though I don't think I ever really understood how to play. I certainly don't now.

I also made my first attempt at horse riding at Mrs Irving's. I was heaved up on an enormous horse, and immediately came down on the other side. I have a mental picture of lying on my back staring up at the blue sky, with this huge mound of horse in the corner of my vision. In accordance with tradition they immediately put me back on again, and I rode a few paces. Later I went some quite long distances on my own, but never really felt at ease. Mule or donkey became a more natural four-legged vehicle for me.

Our biggest adventure was a camping holiday at the end of 1943 in Córdoba – or rather Alta Gracia in the hills to the south west of the city. Our parents were not campers and were a bit apprehensive at taking Jonathan, only eighteen months old, but they were in a strong party of friends – Roger and Carol Minor (experienced campers, my mother assured her mother-in-law) with their three children, Carol's sister Joan Preston with her husband and small boy, and Jack and Winnie McGaull with their son – eight adults and eight children. 'Jack McGaull is a great asset,' wrote my mother reassuringly, 'because he also is a good camper, cook and washer up & very hefty.' We took over the site of a scout camp with its facilities, including two permanent latrines, nicknamed Clementine and Tipperary (the latter, of course, a long way away). We slept under canvas, cooked in the open and generally lived a healthy life. Most of the detail of this memorable holiday comes from photographs and what I have been told. But one memory that must be peculiar to me is the sight of my parents waving to me from the top of a hill. They went off for a walk and suddenly reappeared on a different plane. I had never seen a hill before, Buenos Aires and the surrounding area being completely flat, so could only imagine that they were on an enormous piece of stage scenery, which they had ascended by some stairs at the back.

Aeroplane travel featured at an early stage, since my father sometimes went on business trips by air. Initially we used to go to the airport to meet him on return, but never with any success – his plane was always hopelessly delayed by some mechanical fault or other. So in the end we used to wait at home for him to arrive. Once it was in the early morning, and I was standing on the landing doing my exercises – 'up, down, up, down' – when another voice joined in – 'up, down, up, down!' At first I couldn't think what was happening – my father must have been away for a week or so and I had had time to forget him. When I realised who it was my knees practically gave way under me, so overcome was I with joy at his return.

******

This idyllic childhood unfolded against a background of war. It came close to us just two months after our arrival, when the marauding German pocket battleship *Graf Spee* was trapped by a British fleet in the mouth of the River Plate and scuttled by its captain – the most dramatic naval encounter of the beginning of the war. I have no memory of this, but I do remember British warships docking in neutral Argentina and our entertaining the sailors at the Lomas club and even at home. My mother would later tell us how she once cooked a large joint of the choicest beef, the Argentine staple, for them. After polishing it off, one of them gloomily observed, 'That would have had to last an English family a whole week!' My mother was acutely conscious of the easy life we led in contrast to those back home and when possible sent parcels of food and clothing to help eke out the ration coupons. Mail between England and Argentina did get through, though irregularly, and some of the copious correspondence between our parents and their loved ones at home has survived. Both sides numbered their letters meticulously in series, and much of their correspondence was taken up with guessing the contents of letters that they knew had been posted but had not been received. They were also inhibited, especially on the English side, by the censors. 'It's difficult to write when all we think and talk about is the war and I can't write of that,' wrote my grandmother Nellie. Sometimes we received letters that were just strips of shredded paper, so much had the censors cut out.

My father was equally conscious of being in a safe civilian job when men of his age were serving and dying, and he worried that people at home would think he was shirking. The informal letter he had had from Shell in 1939 was later backed up by an official document from the British Embassy certifying that he had 'offered his services to His Majesty's Government in the United Kingdom for employment in the war effort. It has been decided that he will render the best services by remaining in his present employment with Shell Mex Argentina, Limited.' My father sent a copy of the certificate (signed by His Majesty's Ambassador as well as the Consul General, he emphasised) to his mother so that she could demonstrate to anyone interested that he had volunteered to serve but had been ordered by the Government to stay put.

******

On 3rd August 1944 my father left Buenos Aires on transfer back to Rio. The rest of us joined him in Rio a whole year later, but even then without Robin, whom we left behind at St George's to complete the school year in December. I don't know whether there was any talk of us moving to Rio earlier, but the reasons for not doing so were compelling: as well as having Robin's schooling to consider (he was approaching ten) my mother was some six months pregnant, and a move from our well established home in Temperley would have been very disruptive. Housing was difficult in Rio, to judge by the unsuitable flat where we eventually ended up.

Caroline was born on 27th October 1944. We had been on a visit to Robin at St George's when my mother announced the impending event. Family legend has it that Robin looked displeased. 'Don't you want another brother or sister?' she asked. 'Yes, but not like that – just one after the other! Come on, Martin, let's go and get that ball!' Caroline's birth was less dramatic than Jonathan's. My memories of mother and baby are, I fear, almost entirely eclipsed by those of the fair that was going on in the hospital grounds at the same time. I vividly remember the bran tub, into which you plunged your arm to pick out little objects had been hidden. I pulled out a miniature deck chair, which I treasured for many years. Caroline was christened on Christmas day 1944, when my father was back on leave, in front of a congregation of some three hundred.

We finally flew to Rio to join my father on 3rd August 1945. It was the first time any of us had travelled by air. I don't recall having any qualms before the journey, although for my mother it must have been fraught with difficulty. We cleared right out of Blink Bonnie, down to the last stick of furniture, and then found the plane was delayed twenty four hours, which meant returning to the empty house for a night. When we were finally on the plane pandemonium broke loose. Jonathan screamed his head off, convinced he was going to fall out, I was sick all over the place, and only ten-month old Caroline slept peacefully throughout. Robin was not there to instil order, as he did on later occasions. As we crossed the border between Argentina and Brazil the air hostesses delicately drew the curtains over the portholes, lest we catch sight of Objects of Strategic Importance. When we landed at our first stop across the border, Porto Alegre, we were all finger-printed (all ten fingers), after which my mother had to perform acrobatics to grab her baby and two boys without everyone getting covered in ink. On arrival in Rio we split up for a night or so, presumably because our flat was not ready. I stayed on my own with some friends called Ellis. I was sick again in the lift up to their flat – my father surreptitiously rubbed the resulting mess into the carpet with his shoe. Then I was put to bed with an ice-pack on the back of my neck.

******

We spent only six months in Rio – and Robin less than two months – but to me it was a whole epoch. We lived on the fourteenth floor of a block of flats in Botafogo, in the district of Ipanema (*Rua Senador Vergueiro 232*). It was a nightmare for my parents: water pressure was low, and the lift was frequently out of order. No Victalina this time – I vaguely remember tense scenes when maids were upbraided or dismissed for laziness or dishonesty. And the milk was a curious blue colour, so thoroughly was it diluted with water. It was stiflingly hot, and there was no air conditioning. We children could go out only when accompanied.

Nevertheless, I thought it great fun. For me, the fourteenth floor was itself a mark of status, as well as a privileged vantage point. From the balcony we could look out over Rio bay at Corcovado Mountain, topped by its huge statue of Christ the Redeemer, and at the Sugar Loaf Mountain, with a neon 'Firestone Tyres' advertisement at night. During the day Robin and I would stand for hours watching the aeroplanes come in to land. Some quirk of distance and light flattened the perspective, so that every plane looked as if it was heading straight for the Sugar Loaf. We waited in vain – none of them ever crashed into the mountain. I do recall a plane once flying between the blocks of flats apparently beneath us, which provoked great excitement. There were other, smaller scale excitements. Little Jonathan would lackadaisically throw his toys over the balcony and we would rush to the railings to watch them crash to the ground fourteen floors below.

At this time we used to play Mah-Jong as a regular evening game when my father came home from work. Many years earlier he had bought the set, with its beautiful ivory-fronted, bamboo-backed tiles, as a set of building bricks for Robin, but in Temperley the Platts' delightful Chinese governess Carrie had taught us to play the game, which is similar to rummy. So as to waste no time, Robin would set out the game beforehand. This involved 'washing' the tiles, much as one shuffles a pack of cards, and building them into four 'walls' from which each player would be dealt a hand. Giving an early indication of his mathematical ability Robin once mischievously arranged the game so that Daddy got the highest score possible, and on another occasion so that Daddy didn't get a turn at all. I am sure Daddy quickly understood what was afoot, but he played his part of innocent victim to perfection, to my great excitement and delight.

The only local outings I remember were to the beach, for which we took the Leme Bonde and passed by the hospital where I was born. The most exciting thing about being on the beach was that we were allowed an American ice cream. There were two on sale, Eskibon and Chicabon. I no longer remember what the difference was, but I do remember the agony of having to choose between them. After the swim we would go across the road to the flat of Eddie and Caroline, an American couple, to shower the sand and salt off ourselves and enjoy the luxury of their air-conditioning.

In September or October 1945, before Robin joined us, my father took me on an adventurous trip to stay with my godmother, Ottilie Sherring, who with her husband Ian ran a hotel in Bananal, about half way between Rio and São Paulo. But they lived on a farm high up in the mountains. The first part of the journey we did by car. I almost fell out on a mountain road when I leant on the door handle and opened it by mistake, revealing a yawning chasm underneath me, or so it seemed. Then we transferred to a truck and finally to mules, as wheeled transport couldn't get to the farm. A year later Ottilie wrote to my mother, by then in England, saying she still missed me. Ottilie and Ian had no children of their own, and I can remember no other children on the farm, so I suppose I filled a gap in their life. But I was quite lonely. I have a mental picture of standing rather vacantly among the vegetables on the side of the mountain, oblivious to the spectacular views. At one point I had diarrhoea and made a mess of myself, which was embarrassing. We didn't see all that much of Ottilie and Ian after we left Brazil. At some point they too left Brazil and started various businesses, including an exotic ice-cream parlour in Mozambique and finally a hum-drum café in Winchester, where Robin and I once visited them during school holidays. Years later they were living in what is politely known as 'reduced circumstances' in Putney, from where they wrote to my mother. She must have replied – she always did – but we made no effort to go and see them, which I now bitterly regret.

******

Our second stay in Rio was always meant to be brief. As early as June 1945, while still in Argentina, my mother had written to her mother-in-law asking for advice on our accommodation and schooling back in England. 'Carroll,' she wrote, 'says he has already reserved passages for me and the chaps next April [1946] – though that by no means ensures that we shall travel that month.' There was presumably quite a queue of expatriates waiting to return to England after the war. In the event we secured an earlier passage on the Danish ship *Falstria*.

Although I didn't know it at the time, getting me out of Brazil was quite a business. Because I had been born in Rio the Brazilian authorities claimed me as one of their citizens. At that time they were unwilling to see Brazilians leave the country. My father had to get multiple documents signed. Being the man he was, he marched into the relevant institutions determined to tackle the bureaucracy himself and ignoring the shifty individuals at the entrance who offered, for a fee, to find a way through the labyrinth on his behalf. But eventually he had to give in and hand over to someone who knew whom to bribe and for how much.

Family group: with Mum holding newly born
Caroline, Dad, Robin, Jonathan and Elaine, the girl
next door, Blink Bonnie, December 1944

On 19th January 1946 I was presented with my own Brazilian passport including a page of notes stating among other things that I had to return within two years. A week later I had a British visa in it. I never returned to Brazil.

We left on 7th February 1946, a sweltering day. My father, who again was not travelling with us, checked off our cargo against a printed list, the sweat dripping off his chin and smudging the ink on the papers he was working from. Robin (now aged eleven) was sent running around the ship and into the hold to locate missing items. But once we were under way the voyage was great fun, my third transatlantic trip but the first that I remember. The *Falstria* was a new ship. She had been built in 1940 for the Danish East Asiatic Line to ply the route to Bangkok and was launched in 1941, but war intervened. She was commissioned only in 1945 and used on the more humdrum transatlantic routes (my father spotted her in New York harbour in 1947). She took only 60 passengers, and the Danish crew were kindness itself. My mother always remembered how the ship's doctor came round immediately to inspect her four children. He said he wanted to see what we looked like when we were healthy, so that he would recognise the change if we became ill on the voyage. Robin and I were treated to visits to the bridge by the ruddy-faced First and Second Officers, who were our heroes for months afterwards. All the trappings of a transatlantic voyage of those years were there – the traditional ritual of crossing the Equator involving a sailor dressing up as Neptune, and on our last evening a *dîner d'adieu* with music (including a happy omen in the form of Sibelius' *Finlandia*), for which we still have the menu signed by crew and passengers.

As we sailed northwards it grew colder and colder, until eventually we arrived in Southampton on 21st February 1946. I well remember my first view of bomb-devastated England under a blanket of snow, which I had never seen before. Disembarking was not simple: the *Falstria* dropped anchor in the harbour and we had to board a tender to get to the shore. Then we had to wait hours in a freezing customs shed for our luggage to come through. Poor little Caroline, sixteen months old, got bronchitis as a result.

We had quite a reception committee of grandparents to meet us: my mother's widowed mother Nellie Levi (Grannie to us), my father's parents Colin and Winifred (Grandpa and Grandma), together with Winifred's now widowed sister Ruth Parrott (Great Aunt Ruth), with whom we had spent the day in Clapham at the outbreak of war while waiting for our ship to sail for Argentina. Neither she nor the others had seen us since that time, six and a half years previously, and of course they had not seen Jonathan and Caroline at all. We were the only grandchildren on either side of the family as my father was an only child and my mother's brother and his wife were childless, so it must have a moment of high excitement. They took us to a hotel, where I remember a gas fire and my mother warming a poultice in front of it to apply to Caroline's back. Over-warming, it turned out, and Caroline was burnt. Robin continued to organise us and acquired the title of 'Responsible man No 1' from Great Aunt Ruth. I demanded and was given the title of 'Responsible man No 2' although I am sure I did nothing to deserve it.

After a day or so we left Southampton for Sutton Coldfield, where we were going to make our home for a while in my late Great Grandmother's house. We had exchanged the warm and hospitable climate of our war-time existence in South America for the chilly embrace of post-war austerity England.

Three

Sutton Coldfield: Post-war Austerity

T he house we were taken to in Sutton Coldfield in February
1946 was called Garth, at 15 Boswell Road. Actually it should
have been No 13, a house number that seems to follow us around,
but that number had been erased from the road by superstition. The
house had belonged to my Great Grandmother Julia Levi, who

bought it after she was widowed in 1910 and who had died there in 1944. It had not been my mother's first choice. Writing to her mother-in-law in June 1945 about plans for our return to England she had favoured the Guildford area, as being closer to London and help from Shell: she had to settle her family back in England on her own while Dad remained in Brazil on Shell business. And she was looking for the warmth of the south of England. She had added, as an afterthought, 'There is my Grandmother's house in Sutton available but it is very small'.

To me, and doubtless to my mother, the semi-detached house did indeed feel small, dark and mean, probably because I contrasted it with our fine Blink Bonnie house. Garth was on a steep hill leading down to a railway. The house itself was absolutely standard in design – front and back living rooms, with a passage going through to the kitchen and scullery, which led into a small garden. Upstairs, there were three or four bedrooms, I suppose. Together with the house (it seemed to me) we inherited Mrs Cheeseman, who had 'done' for Julia and now 'did' for us. There were no houses facing it on the other side of the road, but the playing fields of Bishop Vesey's Grammar School, which gave it a pleasant, open feel.

Our time in Sutton Coldfield was one of the bleakest I remember from my early life. It wasn't unhappy, but circumstances were not easy. We had to put up with post-war shortages and rationing, which afflicted everyone but made a particular impact on us, coming as we did from the relative abundance of South America. The winter of 1946-1947 was one of the severest on record. Robin remembers us trying to prise open our frozen coal bunker outside the back door with a screwdriver held in numb fingers under our totally inadequate knitted woollen gloves. A polio epidemic, which peaked in 1947, prevented us going to the cinema for fear of infection, or even to cricket matches.

Above all, my father scarcely figures in my memories of Sutton Coldfield. As far as I can judge from surviving documents he only lived with us for four months out of the nearly two years we were there. Indeed in mid-1947 he wrote to his mother from abroad: 'I've really seen very little of them during the past three years – only four months of Robin and six of Martin apart from odd week ends.' He had joined us from Rio on 5th August 1946, nearly six months after our arrival in England, but he was just on leave, and he was due to return to Rio again in the autumn. He was in an acute dilemma. He couldn't contemplate taking the family back to Rio, nor could he face the thought of another year on his own out there, so on 27th October 1946 (Caroline's second birthday – Dad liked to write significant letters on significant dates) he formally resigned from Shell. In his letter to Jimmy Platt (his former boss in Argentina, now evidently supervising him from London) he acknowledged that

Shell's interests and his own career would best be served by his spending the rest of his working days abroad. He continued:

> After two experiments in Brazil, however, I am not inclined to allow my wife and family to risk a further period there. The improvement in their health and general condition since they have been in England is remarkable and I cannot ignore the fact that I feel quite different myself.
>
> At first I was prepared to continue to live alone in Brazil, but now that my leave is drawing to a close I realise that I cannot face the prospect and that I would be doing neither the company nor myself justice under such circumstances. I have accordingly been making a number of enquiries recently and find that it should not be impossible for me to get a reasonably remunerative job in England and I think that I should therefore tender my resignation herewith.

Had I been privy to these deliberations I would have been surprised, as I had enjoyed our six months in Rio and didn't enjoy the cold in England. But it had been an enervating time for my parents, who found the heat difficult to take, and my mother was very thin when we returned. The alternative my father hinted at in his letter was a teaching job he had been offered (with my mother in tow as a matron or something like that) at his old prep school, Forres, in Swanage on the south coast, where Robin and I were just starting. All our lives would have changed had he accepted it, but Shell was reluctant to lose him, and with a promptness that suggests a bit of pre-cooking Mr Platt replied with the suggestion that my father apply for a London-based job in the Export Department of Shell Petroleum, where he was accepted less than three weeks after his resignation letter.

That didn't mean I saw any more of my father, initially at least. For four months at the turn of the very cold year 1946-1947 he was working at Shell's wartime London office at the Lensbury Club, Teddington, and living in a hotel owned by Shell on Ham Common, Richmond. He only got home for the occasional weekend. Then he had to go abroad again to Central America on a gruelling six-month inspection trip of oil refineries and well-heads between April and October 1947. The trip brought material benefits: unencumbered by rationing, although limited by exchange regulations to £75, which he carefully guarded for five months till he reached New York, he was able to buy clothes for himself and his family, as well as respond to requests from home that took him far beyond his normal shopping range – embroidery silks and fashion magazines for his sister-in-law Bubbles and difficult to obtain cooking utensils for his wife. 'What *is* a sugar thermometer?' he asked pathetically, apparently not knowing whether to look for it in a grocery store, a chemist's or an

Family group, but without Dad:
on the doorstep of Garth, Sutton Coldfield,
September 1947

ironmonger's. In Trinidad, then still British territory, his spending was not constrained, and he ordered food parcels for all and sundry, though local export restrictions meant that they had to be shipped from Australia. Despite these perks, he couldn't wait to get home and settle down with his family.

By this time Robin and I were also away much of the time at boarding school. We had had about three months of idleness when we first arrived in Sutton, and I suppose this was when I missed my father most. In part our time was filled with some remedial teaching at home to make up for our disrupted education. I had been to a nursery school in Buenos Aires, but had had no schooling in Brazil. Robin had stayed on in Argentina to finish his school term, but his education there had been deficient in the history of England. So

Mum hired a good soul to teach us history at home. All I remember is going through a book of stories about various kings and queens, but missing out on the Princes in the Tower because it was 'too sad'. Robin had good Spanish (half his classes in St George's had been in Spanish), so Mum thought it would be a good idea to give him some French coaching. That was a disaster, as Robin couldn't help using Spanish to answer questions put to him in French, until one day he burst into tears and the experiment was ended.

We didn't have friends of our own age in Sutton, and going to boarding school meant we would not acquire any. There was some, mainly adult, society. Sutton Coldfield was our mother's home town. Her widowed mother Nellie Levi was now living in a flat in nearby Four Oaks with her bridge playing friend Mrs Crump, and I remember going to tea there. They were rather stiff occasions – our long absence and her intervening grief must have told on our relationship. Mum's brother Martin Levi lived in Edgbaston, and Robin recalls us going to visit him and his wife Bubbles in their flat in 21 York Road. We would get a bus from Sutton to the centre of Birmingham and then another one out from there. Uncle Martin and Auntie Bubbles were fairly well off – the family firm, Barker Brothers, was doing well exporting silver to the US. Bubbles once took it into her head to send us back with a generous but totally inappropriate gift – a Gorgonzola cheese. We had to carry the smelly thing back on the bus in acute embarrassment as the other passengers, unused to exotic cheeses, strongly advised us to throw it out, as it had obviously gone off. Our doctor Margaret Fairley was an old family friend, and we saw something of her and her two children Richard and Jennifer, though they were too wild for our taste (a common complaint in our well-behaved family). We went to the local parish church, but escaped being recruited into the choir on the valid excuse that we would be absent much of the time.

Despite our rather self-contained life, we always had enough to do to keep ourselves amused. In the first place, we had our routine of household jobs, which included making our own beds, stirring the breakfast porridge and washing up. For that we had a strict division of labour – one of us cleared the table and dried up, the other washed up and put away the dried things. Jonathan and Caroline were too young to do this, but they had some activities: Mum hired a young girl, Miss Clarke, to take them for a walk once a week, and at a certain point they started going to a nursery school at the top of the road. Heartless as it sounds, I don't recall 'the kids', as I called them, impinging very much on our life at that stage. Robin and I played 'Yorkshire cricket' in the back garden. This was a game invented by Robin to ensure that we never hit the ball out of the garden: one was only allowed to bat as a Yorkshire cricketer, i.e. defensively.

We listened to the radio a lot, as did everyone those days, mainly the BBC 'Home Service' (the precursor of Radio 4). *Women's Hour, Children's Hour* and *Listen with Mother* were regulars for the appropriate age groups. For thrills, along with millions of other listeners, we turned to *Dick Barton, Special Agent,* the BBC's first daily serial, broadcast every weekday evening on the 'Light Programme' (the precursor to Radios 1 and 2). Each 15 minute instalment contrived to leave us in agonising suspense over the fate of Dick and his loyal friends Jock (Scots) and Snowy (Cockney). Cricket commentaries were a must. Our musical diet was strictly classical. Dad always recalled with approval how Robin at an early age reacted to his mistakenly tuning the radio to a popular music programme. 'Dat not mugiz, dat lah-di-dah!' he is alleged to have said. On one famous occasion just before Christmas we roasted chestnuts in the fire while listening to Handel's Messiah. In a thank-you letter after Christmas Robin wrote to his paternal grandmother 'We listened to the Messiah eating chestnuts.' She didn't let him forget that. Other concerts we were allowed to enjoy when already tucked up in bed, which was very cosy. So cosy, in fact, that I usually fell asleep in the middle. I was a bit hurt when my mother snapped at me for this habit: 'If I let you listen to a concert in bed it's to listen to music, not to go to sleep!' She was always on a fairly short fuse, 'waxy' we called it. Life in immediate post-war England for a single mother (as in effect she was) with four children was not easy. Robin remembers that when Dad first joined us on his return from Rio Mum laid out a rather festive family meal in the dining room, where we rarely ate. The general enjoyment was brought to a rather sudden end, however, when Mum rebuked Dad for unthinkingly helping himself to a generous hunk of cheese: 'Carroll, you've just eaten one person's weekly ration of cheese!' A most uncharacteristic outburst in front of us children.

When my father was home on leave (16th September 1946 to be precise: the programme is carefully pasted into his album) he took Robin and me to Walsall Town Hall for my first 'live' concert. I had a cold and was desperately worried about coughing, but what really went wrong – it seemed to me – was that at the start of the concert no one came forward to announce the items. I hadn't understood that the announcer I heard on the radio was for us listeners only. The orchestra was the Liverpool Philharmonic under Karl Rankl. The programme, Beethoven's *Leonora* Overture No 3, Elgar's *Introduction and Allegro for Strings*, Borodin's *Dances from Prince Igor* and Tchaikovsky's Fourth Symphony, was a dream programme for my father and an impressive one for me too. I was instructed in particular to note the 'Fate' theme on the trombones in the Tchaikovsky and did so. Robin remembers the middle movement, where the strings are playing *pizzicato* from beginning to end, the sort of detail that intrigued Dad.

We went into Sutton from time to time, shopping. For us that meant a visit to Linda's sweet shop, clutching our ration cards. The town was also a small window on to a wider world. I once saw a German prisoner of war getting on a bus. He was wearing a distinctive black and white striped jacket and trouser suit with POW stamped in large letters on the back. I was told that by then there were quite a few of them around, free in all but name and awaiting repatriation (or marriage in England, which had its attractions).

On one of our shopping expeditions Robin was bought a proper bicycle with gears from the local hardware merchant, B. W. Lee, whom we always called Billy Willy Lee. I had something on two wheels that was decidedly more junior, maybe bought, more likely handed down by someone. I envied Rob's bike with gears and prattled on endlessly, 'I *wish* I had a gear'. We were able to cycle up and down the quiet cul-de-sac that was Boswell Road, as well as in the grounds of Bishop Vesey's during the holidays. Boswell Road was quite steep. Robin remembers the milkman lowering his crates of milk down the pavement on a string during the coldest winter period, unwilling to venture down with his milk float. I remember Robin coming off his bike spectacularly during a too speedy descent. He got a bit of grit lodged in his knee which he has carried there ever since, a sort of memento. We were allowed to take our bikes to Sutton Park, a splendid expanse, with streams (good for Pooh sticks) and a pond (good for sailing model boats), where our mother had skated as a child. There was ice enough during our winter there, but I don't think we attempted skating – we had no skates for a start. Instead we played 'ducks and drakes' – skimming stones across the ice until they crashed (rather dangerously for any casual passer-by) into the further shore.

The final months of our life in Sutton Coldfield in the autumn of 1947 were busy with preparations to move closer to London, although being away at school I knew nothing about it and can only piece together the fragmentary information in some of the fifty six letters (carefully numbered as always) my father wrote from his American trip. He had planned to return with the *Queen Elizabeth* on 23rd September, disembarking at Southampton and seeing Robin and me in Swanage at the start of our term. But the tour overran its original schedule, and he only got back on 8th October, on the Cunard White Star liner *Mauretania*. From then on it was serious house-hunting while we older boys were at school and Jonathan and Caroline were 'parked' in a children's home near Broadstairs (notorious in family annals for housing a bully-boy known as 'the bodger'). The actual move probably took place in early 1948 immediately after the Christmas holidays. I have a clear recollection of being in 15 Boswell Road at a time when all the furniture had gone, and I was able to run my Dinky Toy racing car all the way round the unexpectedly large space of the dining room. This bonus did not compensate for the sadness I felt on leaving surroundings that had become familiar, however bleak they may have seemed when we arrived nearly two years earlier. The sadness did not last, however: by that time I was already spending more weeks of the year at my prep school in Swanage than at home.

Four

Forres: All Things Keenly

I had always expected to go to boarding school and was not overly concerned about it. My parents had both been boarding school children, and Robin had set the pattern for our generation by boarding at St George's in Argentina. For most of my life I have assumed that it had been determined from the start that we boys would go through the same institutions as my father – preparatory school at Forres, public school at Oundle (Bramston House) and University at Cambridge (St Catharine's College). The only child of itinerant and separated parents, my father had made these places his home and remained fiercely loyal to them to the end of his days. But a letter I recently discovered, written by my mother to her mother-in-law in June 1945, shows that while we were still in Argentina and Dad back in Rio, things were far less clear cut. For all she knew Forres had been destroyed or in any case might be too dear.

Forres had not been destroyed. During the war the school had been evacuated to Penn House, near Amersham and the buildings used for radar training, but by the time we arrived the school was back in Swanage. Forres had been founded in 1910 in Northwood, Middlesex, by Arthur and Muriel Chadwick. Dad had time for a few terms there before it moved in 1919 to larger premises in Northbrook Road, Swanage. Arthur Chadwick died shortly after the move and the headship was taken over by his younger brother, the Reverend R. Mackenzie Chadwick ('Mac' to his family, 'Chaddy' to us). Chaddy the younger was still running it some 25 years later, when Robin and I arrived. It was one of a clutch of small prep schools in the area, all of which have now closed or merged. Forres itself was merged with Sandle Manor in Fordingbridge, Hampshire. The site is now a home and school for severely autistic children.

Terms were long, half term being just a weekend during which only a few boys went home. In an average year we spent thirty seven weeks at school against fifteen at home. It's not surprising that I remember a lot of detail about the school, the staff and the boys.

In our days the full postal address of the school consisted of just three words: Forres, Swanage, Dorset. It was easy enough to identify, superbly positioned on the brow of a hill not far from the beach, with a magnificent view of Swanage Bay. The original building had been added to bit by bit. The front door, which I probably only used two or three times during my whole stay, led into a formal hall, but as you went up the corridor (no running or jumping – a punishable offence) you came to the places where we would mill around – the notice boards and the changing room from where we would spill out into the open air, correctly attired, for whatever outside activity was next on the list. More often than not it would just be to hang about on the tarmac during break or to go up to the 'top field' to practise at the cricket nets or kick a ball around.

On the first floor were our dormitories, named after British luminaries from the war – Churchill, Alexander, Portal, Mountbatten and more. There were also bathrooms, of course, pride of place being given to the plunge, of which more below. The first floor also accommodated Matron, a sick room and bed-sitters for single staff. These were their space and we never did more than peep inside.

Forres was run in the tradition of muscular Christianity. There was lots of chapel-going – the school was unusual in having its own chapel. And it was patriotic – we celebrated Empire Day, although the Empire was fast slipping away. Forres had its famous sons, notably Hugh Foot, who became the UK's Ambassador to the United Nations and was ennobled to become Lord Caradon, and his brother Michael, leader of the Labour Party in the early 1980s. Dad admired Hugh Foot, but said rather less about Michael, a *Labour* politician. As I began to be interested in athletics my favourite Old Forresian was Christopher Chataway, who paced Roger Bannister in the first four-minute mile and himself became world 5,000 metres record holder for a brief period.

******

Getting Robin and me settled into Forres in May 1946 was a major undertaking. We were taken by train from Sutton Coldfield to Parkstone, Poole, where we stayed overnight with Mum's cousin James Buchanan and his wife Frankie, who then took us in their car to Forres. We arrived, deliberately, a day before term started and spent the afternoon on the beach with some of the Chadwick family. So Robin and I were somewhat privileged pupils. The reason we were given such a soft landing in Forres was, I suppose, that we had come from abroad and were starting prep school at the age of nearly twelve and nine respectively, against the normal starting age of eight. I certainly found the whole thing pretty bewildering and a bit intimidating. That night we were ushered to the separate dormitories we would occupy: Robin and I were used to sleeping in the same room. So I was all alone in a dormitory designed for twenty or more boys, with Robin way out of reach down the corridor. It was pitch dark when I woke up in the middle of the night with an urgent need to relieve myself. I thought the lavatories were one floor above me. Creeping out into the corridor I could see the light under the study door of the second master, Mr McRae, but nowhere could I find the staircase. I kept bumping into a chest of drawers. Far too scared to knock on Mr McRae's door I crept back to bed and wet it.

My prime concern in the next few days was to make contact with Robin amid the crowd of sixty to seventy boys who had arrived on the official first day of term. Not that I had anything particular to say to him or that I was dependent on him – we had after all led our separate lives for months at a time when he was at boarding school in Argentina – but over the previous three months in Sutton Coldfield we had been thrown very much together, and it seemed unnatural to be in the same place but not to see each other. The opportunities were there: as it was summer term, in the various breaks most of the school would mill around on the 'top field' for fresh air (indeed we probably had to). The problem was, as I pretty quickly realised, that it was 'cheeky' for a younger boy to approach an older one. Everyone knew of course that some boys were brothers, but that was something they did at home, not at school. Luckily Rob found a friend, A. K. D. (Tony) Townsend, who was between our ages and could safely be seen talking to both of us. Not every boy would have been so generous, but Tony had also lived abroad, in Canada, so perhaps felt himself to be a fellow exile returned. We never became close friends, but I do vaguely recall visiting him at home in the Beaconsfield area at some point, and Robin recalls us taking him to a cricket match at Lord's. At all events, he was a 'friend in need'.

After a while we settled down, and Robin and I lived our own lives, though there were certain fixed points when we met. One was when Rob handed me Mum's weekly letter to the two of us. Another, later on in our time at Forres, was when he passed on our weekly copy of the *Eagle* comic, to which Mum subscribed on our behalf. We must also have put our weekly letters home into one envelope, but that might have been done by the staff, since these were not private documents. When Robin left for Oundle I scarcely noticed he had gone – by that time I had my own circle and my own life. And I don't recall paying any attention at all to Jonathan, five years younger than me, when he arrived. By that time I was far too senior. Poor Jonathan, naturally excitable and a bit headstrong, was always being compared unfavourably by the staff to Robin and me: 'Your elder brothers would *never* have done a thing like that!' It doubtless increased his rebelliousness. Robin was Nicholson *ma* (for major), I was Nicholson *mi*[nor] and Jonathan Nicholson *min*[imus]. (In fact we were never all three at Forres together, but after Robin's departure another, unrelated Nicholson popped up in the 'minor' slot, relegating Jonathan to 'minimus'.) We were all called 'Nicky' by staff and fellow pupils alike, as Dad had been in his time. Later, at Oundle, we were all called 'Nick', for exactly the same reason. Tradition counted for something.

I had started in the bottom class, perversely called Form 6, having failed to answer correctly some very elementary questions put to me by Mr McCrae. 'Mac', as he was nicknamed, was a forbidding figure and I probably lost my nerve, having never before been subjected to this sort of interview. After a few weeks I was promoted to Form 5, which was a boost to morale, and from then on school was just a question of getting on with the routine.

The day started with a cold plunge. An outsize bath had been built into one end of the communal bathroom, and we queued up, naked, to jump into the cold water and out again. It was in this plunge that we also took our first swimming lessons, which means it was big enough to accommodate one boy with arms and legs spread out, and therefore several jumping in in quick succession. Matron (Miss Hallam) and her assistant (Mrs Wilson) stood by to dry the littler boys, but the bigger ones were left to look after themselves. We made our own beds with 'hospital' corners. We had a cooked breakfast, after which we had to report that we had performed appropriately in the toilet; otherwise we had a dose of dried figs.

There could be as many as six or seven classes in the day, while on Wednesdays and Saturdays we had sport all afternoon, for which we walked five minutes down the road to the school playing fields. The day's programme was punctuated by non-academic subjects. One of the lessons each day would be gym. In the summer it would be swimming for those who had passed their test – a mad rush down to the sea, changing in the large boat-house, ten minutes in the water, then back again, all within the space of three quarters of an hour, so we arrived at our next class with sand between our toes and behind our ears. There was space for nature study. It was boringly taught, but it did allow us to get to know some of the delights of our seaside surroundings, and I imagine my craze for butterflies began there – the chalky downs were alive with them. There was carpentry, which I enjoyed and which taught me to tuck my left thumb into my palm when sawing. I had failed to do so just before a school play, and I appeared on stage with my thumb heavily bandaged and arm in a sling, feeling like a war hero.

Saturday evening would be special, as there was usually some form of entertainment – a lecture or even a film. Sunday had a fairly tight routine too. There were two services to attend in Chapel – and once a month a communion service before breakfast if you were confirmed. The services were traditional Anglican Morning and Evening Prayer, with no allowance made for our youth. Much of it was gobbledy gook to us – I repeated endlessly a promise to 'stew evil and do good' (the word eschew was not part of my vocabulary). But the atmosphere could be cosy and sometimes moving, as when we raised our voices 'for those in peril on the sea' on a stormy night when you could hear the waves crashing not far away. The process of confirmation (which I must have gone through aged twelve or so) and the communion ritual left me completely bemused, however. I think I once plucked up courage enough to tell Chaddy that I didn't really understand what it was all about, but I can't remember how he replied. The main concern for all of us confirmed boys was how to get through the communion service without falling asleep, keeling over in a faint (we had had a cup of tea but no breakfast) or making slurping noises with the communion wine.

After morning service there was letter writing, which was a highly organised activity. The youngest boys weren't expected to be able to think of anything to say, so prompts – usually the results of the week's sporting activities – were put on the blackboard for them to copy. A typical letter might have read:

Dear Mummy and Daddy

I hope you are well I am. Last week Forres beat Hillcrest We had a Charlie Chaplin film.

Love from ...

At some point in the lower forms (I think it went together with letter writing) we did copybook, in which we copied an elaborate 'looped cursive' style. This was fine so far as it went, but it didn't go very far, since we were not expected to reproduce this style in our ordinary writing, so we just reverted to whatever scribble was most convenient. Copybook was thus more of a penance than a lesson in handwriting. In this way I never learnt a usable style of writing until I took up italic handwriting at Oundle many years later. Poor handwriting and presentation were to plague me (and my teachers) throughout my time at Forres, as my reports show. Even when quite senior I was put on extra copy book in my spare time. I was so embarrassed and ashamed that I tried to do it secretly from my class-mates and fell behind with the exercises. The knowledge that my dereliction of duty would in due course be revealed filled me with fear and completely overshadowed one Christmas holiday, though the staff were kind when I did confess. Aside from style, the process of putting pen to paper was itself complicated enough. The pen was a wooden stick with a nib on the end. You dipped the nib in the inkwell embedded in the right hand corner of your desk, trying to collect sufficient ink to last you a few words, but not so much that the ink dropped off the pen on its way to the paper. If it did, you had to use blotting paper ('blotch'), which didn't erase the ink splodge but at least prevented it smearing the whole page the next time you drew your sleeve across the desk. If your neighbour jogged you by design or accident, ink would splatter far and wide. Our desks were of the traditional gently sloping design. For posture they were in fact very much better than the tables that succeeded them, although they were cumbersome and couldn't be stacked.

After lunch on Sunday came the afternoon walk. In winter it was heralded by the command, 'Caps, macs and outdoor shoes!' Notice that we did not wear gloves. I was always cold in winter and got chilblains on my fingers. I know Mum petitioned for me to be allowed to wear gloves on cold days, but I'm not sure that I ever did. Hot days in summer were just as bad, as we tramped through the back streets of Swanage on our way to Ballard Down, skin itching under our coarse grey flannel shirts. Walks were unpopular, and I remember some boys sacrificing worms to the rain gods in an effort to get the walk cancelled. If it did rain we had a wonderful free afternoon in which to play marbles up and down the long corridors. There was chapel again in the evening and reading last thing. We were read to in smallish groups by one of the senior staff. They would read good stuff – G. K. Chesterton's Father Brown Stories were a favourite of mine. Lounging in Chaddy's or Mac's cosy study, or Mr Strange's drawing room, fire blazing, or on the lawn in summer, devouring our ration of sweets one by one, we enjoyed the one avowedly hedonistic event of the week. It was a bittersweet moment, however, because the next day it would be back to the work routine.

At the end of 1949, when I was already in the top form, I developed a serious aversion to this treadmill and would look at my timetable with loathing: why was I being subjected to this compulsory learning? Other boys in other schools didn't have to do it (not true, of course, but I convinced myself that it was). In my Christmas 1949 report Chaddy wrote:

Occasionally, when things are not quite to his liking a hint of the sea lawyer attitude is apt to appear, and he must try to realize that this does not fit in with his position in the school.

A *what* attitude? Dad explained that it meant someone who tended to find some spurious reason to quibble and to question everything he had to do. The army term was barrack room lawyer. I denied it indignantly, but I knew it was true. I objected to having to take responsibility for things that I had not chosen to do myself – like going to school – but I was basically a conformist and never had the courage to rebel openly. Hence the muttering and grumbling. I can still be like that today.

Another problem as I approached the top form was the onset of short-sightedness. Like most myopic children I wasn't conscious that anything was amiss – I just found it easier to see what was on the blackboard if I looked through a little triangle of light between the thumb and two first fingers of my left hand. I did this instinctively and was most put out when one of the masters implied I was playing the fool. When he realised that I wasn't he made me sit in the front row, which was humiliating, as my position at the top of the class entitled me to sit in the back row. When the holidays came I was taken to a grand place in Kensington to have my eyes tested by the conscientious, generous (she continued to test the family's eyes for free after she had left the National Health) and extremely shy Miss Savory, who had been at Cheltenham Ladies' College with Mum. She recommended Curry and Paxton (now Boots Opticians in Red Lion Street, Richmond, which I still patronise) to prescribe my National Health glasses, which they sent by post to Forres. There was a further humiliation when I had to put them on, as their Harry Potter-ish wire frames were not then the fashion item they would be fifty years later – real men wore horn-rimmed spectacles.

There was *some* free time inside this generally tight programme. We were encouraged to go up to the top field and 'kick a ball around' (which was also the advice given to the older boys who might be experiencing the first sensations of a sexual urge). But we preferred to use the precious moments to indulge in the latest craze, whatever it was. None of us had many possessions, and although some boys were richer than others, money couldn't buy things that weren't available in the shops. Marbles were cheap and easily obtainable, so there were always games of marbles going on up and down the linoleum covered corridors. During most of my time at Forres, Dinky Toys were the real prize. We were not allowed to go shopping ourselves, but whenever it was learnt that the Swanage toy shop had had a delivery of Dinkies the duty master would collect the boys' wish lists, backed by their pocket money, and go off to buy up the shop, more or less. Then for days afterwards we would be admiring our own purchases and envying those of others.

Robin and I found when we arrived that many boys (or rather their parents) subscribed to a comic – *Dandy* and *Beano* were the favourites. I don't know whether we unavailingly urged Mum and Dad to do the same for us or whether our upbringing got the better of us, but in April 1950 the Rev'd Marcus Morris came to our rescue with a superior comic called *Eagle*. He wanted to provide young boys (and their sisters later with *Girl*) with an exciting but wholesome comic, and in this he succeeded – with Dan Dare the space pilot, Harris Tweed the detective and an assortment of other characters that became household names to generations of middle-class boys. There were serious dailies, *The Times* and *The Daily Telegraph*, in the school library, but international affairs scarcely intruded into our life. I remember only the assassination of Mahatma Ghandi on 30th January 1948 by a Hindu extremist (puzzling – how could anyone be more extreme than Ghandi?) and the Korean War, which started in June 1950 and was easier to understand. We followed on maps the worrying contraction of 'our' territory under the onslaught of the Communist North Koreans and Chinese and then, mercifully, its gradual expansion again. I found school library books more absorbing – uplifting historical adventure stories by

G.A. Henty and for contrast Henry Fielding's salacious life of the eighteenth century London underworld figure Jonathan Wild.

******

Team sports were taken every bit as seriously as academic work. In our family cricket was the sport. Dad had enjoyed playing cricket and still did, in the annual 'fathers' match'. Dad and Robin were avid followers of the County Championship and the Test Matches, together with all the cricketing statistics that went with these things and were carefully preserved in Dad's priceless collection of the Wisden Cricketer's Almanac. I tagged along, but my head could never really cope with the statistics and instead was full of dreams of fame as a real cricketer.

My chance came towards the end of my time at Forres when I was selected for the school team in the first match of the term against Hillcrest. To everybody's amazement I stayed and stayed at the crease, emerging with sixty runs to my credit. We won the match easily and I went to bed that night in a haze of glory. It dissipated a few days later when someone let slip that David Lee, our captain, had been fuming all the time I was at the crease. Why? Because I was accumulating my runs so abysmally slowly that there was a danger we would not build up a sufficient total in time for us to bowl Hillcrest out before the match finished. He couldn't wait for me to get out so that a real batsman could go in and score a few quick runs. Hillcrest were known to be the weakest school in the locality. Only then did I realise that their bowling was so pathetic that a tortoise would have stayed at the crease as long as I did. In the next match I scored a respectable fifteen, but thereafter hardly a run, until I was dropped from the team. That meant that my dream of playing against Dad in the fathers' match, which crowned the summer term, was shattered, one of the bitterest disappointments of my early life. Happily, everyone around me, masters, boys and parents, was careful not to exploit my humiliation, and somehow I was even put into white flannels – reserved for the school team – for photographs. At the end of that term Chaddy's entire report on me was devoted to cricket:

I am sorry his keenness to master the art of batsmanship has not met with greater success – more attention to his footwork would make a great difference.

In the autumn term we played rugby football, or rugger, as we called it. Rugger meant something to me, since we had come to live in Twickenham, 'the home of rugby', but I have scarcely any recollection of playing it at Forres. In the term after Christmas we played association football, soccer. For some reason it was decided at an early stage that I would be a goalkeeper. It was a miserable position. I had to stand for hours, getting colder and colder while play was at the other end of the field, then spring into action when the players suddenly came thundering towards me and took a shot at my goal. I usually failed to stop the ball, or if I did, my clearance kick was so feeble that it hardly relieved the situation at all. One day after a game I overheard a group of boys dissecting my performance, unaware that I was in the changing room behind a set of lockers. 'He can't even punt, just does feeble drop kicks to clear' (that was true). I was upset, not because they found my performance feeble – I knew it was – but because I was being criticised for not doing well at something I had never wanted to do at all. Stung by this, I demanded to be released from my goal-keeping purgatory. I was told I could play in a different position so long as I accepted that I would be relegated to a more junior team. I was more than happy, and ended my soccer career at Forres running around fairly aimlessly among younger boys, but at least not getting quite so cold. 'Too small to find a place in the team as a goalkeeper but shows promise as a forward' was the generous verdict of Gerald Newton, our coach, in my report.

There was a squash court in the school grounds, but most of us never got near it. Individual sports were not encouraged (there was a good, practical reason too: poorly co-ordinated little boys like us would soon have been crowning each other with flailing squash racquets in that enclosed space). But the school did promote one individual sport: boxing. Boxing lessons alternated with gym, and both were run by a powerful but gentle ex-serviceman, himself an

Cricketers: with Dad and Robin,
wearing those coveted white flannels

amateur boxer, who would show off his bruises after a fight (which we never saw). We learnt how to 'lead with the left' and 'keep your guard up' and punched our teacher or a punch bag for practice. But once a term, or possibly once a year, there was a boxing competition. Misery reigned in the school the day the lists of whom you were to fight went up on the notice board. There was a double fear – fear of being mashed by your first round opponent, and fear of surviving that only to be mashed in the second round, and so on. Pretty well everyone in the school had to take part, so we were divided into several groups. The early rounds of the competition went on throughout the day, during classes. You would be trying to absorb the latest mathematical equations when you were called out of class to spend three or four minutes in the ring (it seemed ages) sparring away as best you could. You then went back to equations, red faced and rumpled, and possibly holding back tears. Most boys hated boxing, and I recall one year when there was a lot of murmuring and talk of a collective refusal to fight. Chaddy got wind of this and did what he always did when faced with this sort of general misbehaviour – he called us into his study individually. There he lectured us on the virtues of boxing – teach you to be a man, valuable lesson in self-defence and all that. And so the competitions went on. One year for some reason I actually won a fight. The congratulations went to my head, and I decided I enjoyed boxing after all. In my next fight I beat Oliver, quite a sporting type, and reached the semi-finals of my group, whereupon I met O'Hanlon. This was a different matter, because we both knew that the winner would have to face Oliphant, a cheery redhead, son of a vicar, who was effortlessly good at all sports and was set to knock the daylights out of either of us. O'Hanlon and I parried around each other endlessly, trying not to land a blow, until our coach realised what was going on and extended the fight round after round until one of us was deemed to have got an advantage. It was O'Hanlon, and I retired relieved. But there is a sting in the tail of that story. The school was suddenly hit by an epidemic of mumps or something like that, and closed before the end of term, so the final never took place. I realised with some bitterness that had I beaten O'Hanlon I would have taken my place in history as the boy who might have beaten Oliphant, without ever having been put to the test. But there was no way back.

******

Cubs, and later Scouts, were halfway between sport and free time. They were voluntary, but if you didn't join you went on a walk on Friday afternoons, and that was sufficient incentive for most of us to join. None of us much liked the Cubs. The uniform was a tickly green sweater and the ritual a bit childish even at our tender age. Our cub mistress was Akela the wolf from Rudyard Kipling's Jungle Book, to whom we Cubs vowed to do our best on every occasion:

Cub Mistress: 'Will you dyb, dyb, dyb?' [do your best]

Boys (saluting): 'A-ke-la, we will dob, dob, dob!' [do our best].

But we had to go through Cubs to get into Scouts, which was altogether different. Scouting derived from the Boer War, and the Scouts' uniform, as exciting as the Cubs' was boring, resembled a sort of safari suit – a khaki shirt with all manner of pockets and shoulder straps, on which our proficiency badges were sewn as we earned them. Round our neck we had a green scarf with a leather toggle. Trousers (still the usual grey shorts, alas) were held up by a belt with a clasp in the shape of the Scouts' *fleur-de-lys* symbol and socks by natty green garters with tabs. On our head we wore a splendid, broad brimmed bushman's hat. We didn't own all this kit; it was recycled when boys left, and all the proficiency badges were carefully unpicked by Matron or some other devoted soul. Nor did we wear it for everyday scouting, but that made it the more desirable. To complete the kit we each had a stave – a five foot long stick marked off in feet and inches and decorated with various symbols. Staves were very much part of everyday scouting – lashed together with sisal (tough, hand-lacerating string) and using the correct knots of course, they could be used to construct everything from a makeshift stretcher to an even more makeshift bridge over a stream. On Friday afternoons we would go up to the Scout Room at the end of the gym over the carpentry shop. Mr McCrae was our principal scoutmaster, assisted by Messrs Peter Chadwick (Chaddy's son) and Gerald Newton. We would always be learning something for a test – knots, first aid, semaphore and/or Morse code. From the Scout room we had a good view of the bay. Every now and then a warship would be at anchor there, and Peter Chadwick (ex-Navy) would negotiate an exchange of flashed Morse code messages after dark. This was tremendously exciting, but showed up our dismal technique – the sailors on board had been asked to keep their speed down to an absolute minimum, but were still far too quick for us to follow them. In summer we would be out laying trails and constructing rickety towers out of our staves. Many was the valiant scout who climbed such a tower from which to semaphore to some distant place, only to be engulfed after a few vigorous arm motions in a heap of collapsing staves and fraying sisal. I passed all my proficiency tests and became the proud leader of one of the four patrols, each of which had its own den in a corner of the scout room. True, it was the Cuckoos patrol rather than the Bulls, but no matter.

The high point of the scouting calendar was the summer camp – a week under canvas in what seemed a very remote place, but was probably a nearby farmer's field just across Ballard Down. The scouts had four or five army surplus bell tents which were taken out each year and tested on one or two exciting evenings before the end of term on the top lawn. We went to camp straight after the end of term, when we were joined by a few Old Forresians down from their Public Schools to relive the old days, and show off. I went to at least one camp from Oundle. In camp we followed routine and discipline as strictly as at school, but it was all so much more fun, even digging the latrines. We dug a long straight trench (our experienced scout masters knew how long it would have to be to accommodate us for a week), carefully piling up the soil behind it, separately from the turf. We made a moveable framework of staves covered with hessian for privacy and moved it the necessary number of paces along the trench at the end of every day. In the mean time everyone using the latrine would replace the soil over their business,

Boy Scout: in full kit on my way to Scout Camp. I am
standing in front of the veranda at Warwick Lodge

and at the end of camp we would replace the turf. Not being in the
habit of squatting *à la française* we must have had a moveable stool
as well. For accommodation, each patrol put up its own tent and then
dug a sizeable trench all around it, with runaway gulleys at the lower
points. Those who skimped were reminded of it when it first rained,
and water trickled, or gushed into the tent. We did all our own
cooking on outside fires with twigs gathered from surrounding
woods, eating and drinking from an assortment of tin and enamel
cans. In the evenings we drank cocoa and sang songs around the
camp fire. The idyll was real.

As scouts we paid lip service to scouting as a national and
international movement. Our group was called something like 3rd
Swanage (Forres) Scouts, so in theory we were one of a broader

group based in Swanage. But we never did anything jointly with the other Swanage groups, let alone participate in the big scouting Jamborees. Scouting was just another school activity, albeit (for me at least) much more enjoyable than most. We didn't take kindly to sharing our activities with boys who were different from us, and when Peter Chadwick, at that time training for the priesthood and running a youth group in London's East End, brought a group of his charges to join us at camp, we greeted them with considerable apprehension. Nor can I report that at the end of a week under canvas we parted with a better knowledge and appreciation of each other. The social gulf was too wide to be bridged. We didn't think of the scouts outside the school context, and Robin and I were once taken by surprise during the holidays when one of the staff at Marble Hill Park, Twickenham, where we were booking a tennis court, seized us enthusiastically by the left hand and announced, 'I was a skate, and my son is a roller skate!' It slowly dawned that he had spotted the scout badges in our lapels, had proffered the left-handed scouting handshake and said, once we had deciphered his (non-local) accent, 'I was a Scout, and my son is a Rover Scout' (a senior scout). Some time after I left scouting declined and was eventually abandoned in favour of other Friday afternoon hobbies, such as photography. The enthusiastic staff who ran it went their separate ways.

My attitude to our activities and to the school itself was largely defined by my view of the staff. I once asked Dad whether he had liked Arthur Chadwick, his headmaster, who solemnly gazed at us from his portrait in the dining room as we ate. He replied, 'Well, he wasn't exactly a person one *liked*.' I was pleased to hear that, because it reflected my feeling towards R. M. Chadwick, Arthur's brother and my Headmaster. He seemed very old, and I suppose he was in his sixties at least, since he retired soon after I left. He always wore his clerical dog-collar; his head had more or less sunk into it and his jowls spilt over its sides. In a hierarchical and dynastic system he represented the ultimate Authority, and didn't need to do anything to maintain it. He may have taken some Scripture classes and of course he ran the chapel services, but otherwise his role was limited to ex-cathedra statements and private interviews with boys who needed to be encouraged, warned or beaten with one of the array of canes he kept behind his door. There were no qualms about corporal punishment in those days: 'getting the stick' was a normal part of school discipline, and Chaddy administered the punishment in the best 'this hurts me more than it hurts you' tradition. I never 'got the stick' – from Chaddy or from any other master, something of which I was rather ashamed, because it made me look like a 'goody-goody'. I wasn't – I was just naturally disciplined and unadventurous. But my one-to-one interviews with Chaddy were seldom satisfactory. One was the boxing lecture. Another was when it was discovered that the bigger boys had started indulging in horse play – lunging at each others' 'privates'. Chaddy once again had us all in one by one to find out if we were partaking in this sport and why. I wasn't and felt aggrieved at the suspicion.

One interview that really upset me was when I went to take my leave before going off for a couple of days to Oundle to sit the scholarship exam. Mum had found a pair of long grey trousers for me for that term, as I was determined not to turn up at my future public school in little boys' shorts. So there I was in Chaddy's study feeling very grown up in my green blazer and grey flannels. Chaddy was furious: long grey trousers belonged to a suit; you couldn't wear them with a blazer! Humiliated, I had to change back into my shorts, which apparently did go with a blazer. Luckily, I was breaking my journey at home. After a fruitless search among Robin's cast-offs for a grey jacket that would go with the grey flannels and thus form a suit, Mum connived at my little disobedience and I set off for Oundle once again in my blazer and long greys, safely out of Chaddy's reach. Only many years later did I dimly understand that Chaddy's objections centred around the English convention that a blazer or sports jacket with flannels signified sport or some other relaxation – you just couldn't sit for a scholarship in such attire.

My final interview with Chaddy was excruciatingly embarrassing, since it was about sex. It went something like this:

Chaddy: You've got a sister, haven't you, Nicky?

Me: Yes, sir;

Chaddy: Well, you know, then, that girls are different from boys ... er ... *down there*!

Me: (reddening): Er .. yes, sir;

Chaddy: Well, from now on you might find that you are beginning to get feelings down there that you haven't had before. You know what you should do if you feel that way?

Me: No, sir;

Chaddy: *Get outside and kick a ball around!* And whatever you do, don't start playing with your privates – that way you can go mad. You know, half the prison population in Britain consists of people who've gone that way.

Me: (a late developing thirteen year old, by now completely flummoxed): Yes, sir. I mean, no sir!

I got the impression from conversations many years later that Chaddy really had been past it in my time. Shortly after I left there was a dreadful tragedy: a group of boys on the Friday afternoon 'non-Scouts' walk accidentally set off an unexploded mine that had been washed up on the shore. Six (I think) were killed. Chaddy was completely paralysed by the tragedy and unable to respond to it in any way.

Next in the hierarchy came Mr McCrae, a dour Scot from a Presbyterian (or stricter) upbringing. He was also a very distant figure. In a rare revelation of something of himself he once told us how as a child he would have to spend all Sunday in bed with only the Bible for company. To have got out of bed would have exposed him to the risk of breaking some Sabbath rule, so it was better to do absolutely nothing. Everything he did was accurate and precise. On weekdays he wore a sports jacket and on Sundays he wore a suit. Appropriately, he taught Maths. Once when he was sitting alone at the senior staff table at lunch we could see he was engaged in some mind game – it turned out he was seeing how accurately he could count 60 seconds before looking at his watch. The secret, he said, was to say to yourself, 'one, Kodak, two Kodak etc.' This was in the days when photographers timed their own exposures, and Kodak had cleverly exploited it. Having learnt it from Mac, I still while away the time waiting for a train matching my seconds, 'one, Kodak, two, Kodak', to those of the station clock. Another of Mr McCrae's maxims that I still try to observe was 'd. i. n.' – do it now. On the whole we found him strict but fair.

Then came J. P. A. (John) Strange, who had on his side youth, a certain worldliness (his mother was from Luxembourg) and a beautiful wife. I don't think that initially he was a very accomplished teacher – he got under my skin at an early stage when he asked us as a class to write on a piece of paper the French words for 'yes', 'no' and 'thank you'. Most of us made a hash of the exercise and were treated to a lecture on how we should know better after x months of learning French. I felt unjustly accused: if we didn't know these things it was because we hadn't been taught them, and anyway the French for 'thank you' was tricky, as we were constantly being told that *merci* could also mean 'no thank you'. What I didn't appreciate was that Mr Strange (like Peter Chadwick and Gerald Newton) had come to the school more or less straight out of uniform and had no training in the finer skills of schoolmastering. Dad would have been in a similar position had Shell accepted his resignation. Mr Strange had been a prisoner in Italy for much of the war and had escaped twice. It was not done to go into details, but this was enough to make him a romantic figure. He and his wife Ena had a little cottage just outside the school grounds and on occasions in the summer term he would take a senior class there to sit in the garden for Latin, which sometimes ended in his declaiming reams of Latin verse in a sort of sing-song Italian. Incomprehensible, but different. He never taught me to love Greek, however, perhaps because he never succeeded in explaining why I should be learning it, aside from adding another string to my bow in the forthcoming scholarship exam for Oundle.

Mr [Edwin] Farwell ('Ruddy' to us, on account of his shining bald pate) was the music master. He also had a cottage in or near the grounds, but he was a widower, whose unmarried daughter kept house for him. He was another of the more austere and unapproachable teachers, and ill-tempered at that. We were always hearing him bark 'ketchup!' ('Catch up' in fact) to boys lagging on Sunday walks. He did everything in the music line, from training the choir and playing the organ in chapel, through producing school concerts and the annual musical play. I loved taking part in the play, almost always a heavily edited Gilbert and Sullivan, with all the dressing up (and make-up on the night) that it involved. I was not in the least abashed by having to play women's parts. Indeed at one point I even had dreams of becoming an actor, until Dad wisely revealed my ambition to Cyril Luckham, a contemporary of his and a moderately successful actor, who firmly advised me against.

Piano was an extra, and Dad, who always wished he had had some musical education, cheerfully paid for it. I made very little progress. I would while away my allotted practice time in some cold dormitory while everyone else was enjoying themselves (I assumed) and then perform miserably in my nervousness during the lessons. Mr Farwell didn't realise that to kindle my enthusiasm he should have got me to play some recognisable tune with both hands. That would have given me something to build on. Instead, it was Beethoven's *Für Elise* ('Furry Lisa'), endlessly, first on the right hand then the left, with no hope of putting them together, as after a while they only seemed to make sense on their own. Mozart sonatas received the same treatment. Mr Farwell would nag away behind me, dropping ash on my shoulder (there were no smoking bans then) until one day he lost patience and said, 'Oh come on, Nicky, Mozart wrote this when he was nine, and you can't even play it when you're thirteen!' Perhaps I should have been flattered that Mozart's musical progress and mine were being viewed through the same lens, but for me it was the last straw.

Chaddy's son Peter taught for a few terms, left to study for the priesthood and returned again towards the end of my time at Forres. When I was old enough to take an interest in these things I began to realise that Peter was being groomed for the headmastership. Forres was a Chadwick family business, and it had been laid down somewhere that the headmaster had to be both a Chadwick and ordained. In the eyes of us ten to twelve year-olds, Peter Chadwick lacked the necessary *gravitas* to be a priest. He had been in the Navy during the war; he had played rugby for Rosslyn Park, a club I knew because it was in Barnes, near our Twickenham home; and he epitomised the Forres motto *All Things Keenly* (*Omnia Studiose*). He could be a terrible nuisance in this *persona*, relentlessly urging us to 'get outside and kick a ball around' whenever he found us looking remotely lethargic. But it also meant that he encouraged activities that were outside the standard curriculum, like recorder groups, which I joined, albeit a little reluctantly, laying the basis for my later flute playing. On the whole Peter Chadwick was a Good Thing, and I was surprised to find myself embracing him with real warmth when we met in October 2002 at John Strange's memorial service.

Peter Chadwick's *alter ego* at Forres was Gerald 'Nutty' Newton, with whom he seems to have had connections in the Navy. They engaged in endless jokes, pranks and witticisms with each other, which we of course enjoyed. Nutty Newton taught geography, in which, I suspect, he had no formal education at all. His teaching left me with the ineradicable impression that geography is for dunces (this stood me in bad stead when I went to St Catharine's College, Cambridge, a 'geography' college). I had the feeling even as a small boy that beneath the banter Nutty was an unhappy man. At one point he got engaged to a nice girl in the kitchen staff, but it was called off. After I left, Nutty Newton did get married, but not long after died suddenly of a heart attack on the squash court.

Mr Forte came somewhat late into my time at Forres to teach French. He was painfully shy and retiring, the most colourless member of staff I can remember. It was he who led the walk that ended with the tragedy of the mine explosion, and no doubt he was consumed by guilt that he had let it happen, though I don't think any blame attached to him. He donated a photography laboratory to the school some years later. Forms 5 and 6 were taught by ladies, Mrs Peacock and Miss Edmonds, when I arrived. I remember Mrs Peacock only as a comfortable sort of woman. Miss Edmonds was a dry and withdrawn lady who taught us natural history, one eye hidden behind a frosted lens of her spectacles. She was replaced by Miss Milligan, young and exciting, with frizzy hair, who later married Peter Chadwick.

At one point Mr Haddock briefly burst into our lives. Whatever he did, he inspired us, effortlessly epitomising the school motto. We were heartbroken when he suddenly announced he was leaving, and felt betrayed when he revealed that teaching had just been a temporary job, between university and a real job, and anyway he had to be nearer his invalid mother. We couldn't imagine that someone who seemed to put his whole being into caring for us could find anything better to do, and his poor invalid mother's ears must have burned. A number of us pooled some of our pocket money to buy him a set of tennis balls as a leaving present. This was not an entirely altruistic gesture; it was intended partly as a demonstration to the rest of the staff that they didn't measure up to this *parvenu*.

Matron was Miss Hallam, strict and impersonal. Her assistant was Mrs Wilson, a war widow, whose son Paul was at the school. Mrs Wilson always cried at the Remembrance Day Service. We all knew that, and those bold enough to cast a surreptitious glance behind them during the service would later confirm: Mrs Wilson was crying. Our horizons were too narrow for us to be touched by the reasons for her crying. In the kitchen were Marsh and Cull, without the 'Mr', I think, as they were definitely 'below stairs' people. They were not cooks, more like butlers/waiters, smartly dressed in black coats and pin-striped trousers. Marsh was a very neat little man, Cull less so, and somewhat sullen. Rumour had it that he voted Labour, which to us sounded much the same as saying today that he had Al-Qaeda sympathies. But he was a kind man, and would cheerfully fry up for our breakfast the mushrooms that we had collected on an autumn morning from the school playing fields.

******

When I look at school photos or lists of boys who were roughly my contemporaries at Forres I can instantly put names to faces and faces to names. It's not surprising: I spent twice as much time with them as with my own family. And we had no private place to which we could withdraw: we were a crowd from start to finish. On the whole we didn't make close or exclusive friendships, nor did we divide into tribes or gangs. We rubbed along with whomever we sat next to at table, in the classroom or in the dormitory. And there was no choice – these places were strictly allocated. Sometimes a shared hobby or craze made for a temporary friendship. For a time, and for inexplicable reasons, Farrant and I shared a passion for motorcycle dirt track racing. Of course we never went near a dirt track, but we had some books and photographs, and perhaps toy bikes. What intrigued me endlessly about this sport was the way the wheels of the bikes turned in the opposite direction to the way the bikes were turning. It didn't happen that way on my bicycle. I'm not sure that I ever understood that they were deliberately skidding round the corners. At another time I found myself always reading the same books as Roger Clarkson Webb. We were 'twins' – born on the same day – and sat next to each other in Form 1. I recall us giggling over a book we were reading, prompting this exchange:

Mr Strange: What are you two giggling about?

Us: The book we're reading, sir.

Mr S: What book?

Us: *With the Corners off*, sir.

Mr S: With the what??

Us: *With the Corners off*, sir. It's about someone's adventures.

Mr S: Sounds pretty silly to me.

Us: (smugly): We got it from the school library, sir!

Mr S: Oh, I suppose it's all right, then.[1]

One of my friends towards the end of my time at Forres was D. M. (David) Lee. We shared a love of cricket – but he was a real

---

[1] It was Commander A. B. Campbell's *With the Corners Off: My Adventurous Life on Land and Sea*, published in 1937. It is described as '*the adventurous life of a man who roamed the wildernesses of Canada and North Africa before WW1. He served in mine-sweepers and armed merchantmen in various theatres*'. The sort of book I (and I suppose most boys) loved.

sportsman. He was the cricket captain who had despaired at my 'epic' innings against Hillcrest. Despite that, he invited me to stay for a few days one summer at his home in Somerset. We watched some cricket. Although Middlesex was 'our' county and I had also adopted Sussex in order to differentiate myself from Robin, I had a soft spot for Somerset, regularly at the bottom of the County Championship, because my godfather Dick Burrough occasionally played for them. We also watched some tennis, because David's father was umpiring. Quite a few years later he hit the national press in a rather unfortunate way – he was photographed fast asleep while umpiring a Wimbledon match. I felt sorry for David. When not watching cricket or tennis, David and I played a sort of touch rugby on the lawn with the family dog, which had developed quite an impressive ability to swerve out of a tackle. I was also introduced to cider – inexplicably considered to be a suitable first alcoholic drink for children. It made me rather ill.

Another of my friends as a more senior boy was J. J. (Jonathan) Chadwick. He was a popular boy (partly because his name gave him lustre – he was Arthur Chadwick's grandson) with a moon face and cheerful demeanour. But one day as we were washing dishes (we did this sort of chore on a rota) he said to me that he was sorry to be leaving Forres without any real friends. I suppose he was showing the first signs of teenage *angst*. I was puzzled, because I hadn't yet reached that stage myself and just took anyone I happened to be next to as my friend, 'real' or not. Many years later Jonathan and I turned up together at St Catharine's College, Cambridge. He had also done National Service, in the army in Cyprus, which brought him close to the Suez war. I was pleased to see him at Cath's and thought that now we really would strike up a friendship, but it was not to be. He was quite withdrawn, and we didn't have much in common: neither of us at the age of twenty was much inclined to spend hours mulling over our prep school days. He was later to hold a senior position in the Imperial War Museum.

Not every boy was happy at Forres. One, Markby, even ran away. I think he just went home, his father being a prominent local surgeon. There was Jennings, a bully. He was large for his age, not clever, and I think we understood that he was basically insecure. And there were two under-size boys, Firth and Knight, who were always put upon. Oddly enough, it was again at university that I came across Tim Knight's sister Judith. It was a relief to hear from her that her brother didn't show any signs of having been badly treated at Forres; my conscience told me that he had.

The oddest boy in my time was Christopher Lambert. A couple of years older than me Lambert always looked as if he was completely new to the school. He never got the hang of our routine-based, disciplined life and was forever getting into trouble, piling up BCMs (Bad Conduct Marks) at a staggering rate. He looked different, too, having had an operation for a tubercular gland that had left a scar around his throat and gave him a prematurely aged appearance. We all knew that he was special, because his father was Constant Lambert, the composer of *Rio Grande* (which for some reason we all knew, or thought we knew). Chaddy seemed to enjoyed publicly humiliating him, even when ostensibly praising him. At the end of one term in his usual summing up speech Chaddy said: 'And this term has been special in one further way – Lambert didn't get a BCM!'

But worse was to come. Surprisingly for such a disciplined school, it was accepted that we all defaced the school text books (there was no *Shorter Latin Primer* to be found: they were all *Shorter Eating Primer(s)*). I used to draw elongated men in top hats (for reasons unknown). One day the top three classes were summoned by a grim faced Chaddy, supported by senior staff. Chaddy said that dirty pictures had been drawn in some text books, and he was going to make an example of the principal perpetrator – Lambert. To general amazement and horror he called Lambert up, bent him over a chair and proceeded to give him a public beating (beatings were usually administered in the privacy of Chaddy's study). Lambert made to get up after four strokes, but was told to bend down again for the full six. For good measure, we were all declared to be complicit, and the school outing to *The Mikado* was cancelled as a punishment. Having no idea of what a 'dirty' picture would even look like, I was bewildered and angered by the humiliation visited on poor Lambert and by the loss of our outing.

Decades later I learnt from a three-generation biography of the Lamberts by Andrew Motion, later Poet Laureate, that Lambert was actually related to the Chadwicks.[2] During the war, as his parents' marriage was foundering, he was frequently parked with his father's cousin Audrey, Jonathan Chadwick's mother and Chaddy's niece by marriage. Chaddy's cruelty towards him may have been designed to avoid showing family 'favouritism', but I think it more likely that Chaddy simply couldn't cope with someone so brilliant and unconventional. Kit (as he became) Lambert went on to become manager and producer of the rock and roll band, The Who, and founder of the first successful independent record label, Track. According to Andrew Motion he 'profoundly affected the course of popular [musical] taste'. He died of accumulated alcohol and drugs in 1981.

******

Parents tended to appear at half term, but otherwise were not much of a feature at Forres. In those days the point of boarding your child was to let the school take over. My impression has always been that my parents were very rare visitors indeed, but the facts belie that: the programmes of school concerts and plays carefully pasted into Dad's

---

[2] Andrew Motion, *The Lamberts: George, Constant and Kit*, London: Chatto & Windus, 1986

album show that he at least attended every school concert but one (always in the last week of June) between 1946 and 1951, and three school plays or operettas. Moreover, in June 1947, while Dad was on his extended tour of Central America, Mum came down with Jonathan and Caroline for a week's holiday, when she was generously made welcome by the Chadwick family.

A special visit came in October that year when quite early one morning Chaddy summoned Robin and me to his study and told us conspiratorially that we should go down to the Wolferton Hotel, which stood on a corner not far from the main drive down from the school, where a surprise awaited us. It was Dad, who had just returned by ship to Southampton from his tour and with Mum had seized the opportunity to visit us. We each came away with a Queen Elizabeth (the ship) souvenir propelling pencil, to the admiration and envy of our school mates. It was my most treasured possession for many years until I fiddled with it once too often.

It must have been when Jonathan came to Forres that Mum and Dad started coming down to the Wolferton regularly for a week's summer holiday, bringing Caroline. On one of those occasions they walked up the school drive in holiday attire, which meant Mum in trousers – for the first time ever, as far as we were concerned. Family annals have it that a horrified Jonathan exclaimed, 'Mummy, those trousers – take them off!' Had I been a little older I might have been embarrassed at having my parents

On Swanage beach: with Caroline and Jonathan,
June 1947. Behind us is the Forres boat-house

around during term time, but it was fun to see them and Caroline installed on the beach when our class went down for our hasty swim.

On those occasions when Mum and Dad did not come down for half term, I was often taken out by other boys, but my happiest memory is of the occasion when I was the only boy not being taken out. I was perfectly content in my own company, curled up in the library with an adventure book or a bound volume of old *Punch* magazines, anticipating the meal that Cull or Marsh would serve for me and me alone. But the luxurious solitude was to be replaced by something even better. Peter Chadwick was striding down the corridor past the library when he must have seen me out of the corner of his eye. He stopped and popped his head round the door:

People not down, Nicky? (The Chadwicks always called parents 'your people')

No, sir

Nobody taking you out?

No, sir

Like to come sailing with us?

Er, yes please, sir

Within minutes my lunch had been transformed into sandwiches, and we were on our way to get out the dinghy that lived in our large bathing hut, Peter Chadwick, Jill Milligan (whom Peter was courting, but I didn't know that), Gerald Newton and I. That was an adventure in itself, but even better was when we all gathered in the Trocadero for Knickerbocker Glories – an ice cream made up of different coloured layers in a tall glass flute. And even better was to be sitting hobnobbing with the staff under the curious and envious (I was sure) gaze of other boys out with their dull parents (the Trocadero was probably the only café in Swanage at the time, so it was well-populated with half-term parties). And even better than that was to be the centre of attention next day, recounting the outrageous things Peter Chadwick and the others had said in unguarded moments.

I left Forres in the summer of 1951, just approaching my fourteenth birthday, with a good final report, but having failed to get that scholarship to Oundle – maybe I was wearing the wrong trousers after all. I have mixed feelings about Forres, but the balance is on the good side. *All Things Keenly* was a simple but effective school motto, which I have tried to practise ever since.

Memories of Childhood

Five

Warwick Lodge: A Home of Our Own

In April 1948 Robin and I returned from Forres for the Easter holidays to a new home. It was a substantial, detached house, built in 1867, with large bay windows and an imposing front porch supported on two stout pillars. It had been called Warwick Cottage, but nothing could have been less cottage-like, so my parents quickly renamed it Warwick Lodge. It was at 13 Ailsa Road, St Margaret's-on-Thames, then as now a choice residential area set between Twickenham and Isleworth, on the other side of the river Thames from Richmond. This was to be our family home until Mum's death in 1993. As soon as Dad had secured his London-based job with Shell the search for a house was on. It had been complicated by his being away once again, on his six-month tour of Central America. Mum looked at places in Ashtead, Sunningdale and Guildford, while Dad agonised in his letters over finance. In the end they decided that the house had to be within easy reach of the Lensbury Club, Teddington, where Shell were likely to have their London headquarters for some time. So when the estate agent recommended a house in St Margaret's ('I think you'll like this one, Mrs Nicholson'), they snapped it up. It had the right feel, despite having four bedrooms rather than the five they had stipulated. Dad bought it on 10th December 1947 for £4,750 with a loan from the National Provincial Bank. We children sold it after Mum's death in 1993 for £430,000. In 2006 it was again on the market, with an asking price of close on £2,000,000.

With the house came Mrs Williams. She had cleaned for the previous owners, the Lays, who were emigrating to South Africa. She lived in Isleworth, where she did all the necessary for her husband and three children, then cycled over some three days a week to clean and wash for us, stopping off at another house on the way once a week to polish their brass door knob. She was hard-working and totally loyal and became as much 'family' as the class divide of the time allowed. For a time her son Peter was the first call for Warwick Lodge building and plumbing. She remembers Dad and Mum (in a mulberry-coloured outfit with hat) viewing the house, while she, Mrs Williams, tried to keep the Lays' son Paul out of the way. She also recalls the Lays moving out to a hotel so that we could move in. For the first month Dad, back at work in Lensbury, occupied it on his own, living rather primitively and drinking tea with Mrs Williams out of the only vessels available – jam jars.

The house was spacious but initially fairly spartan. It had suffered when a bomb exploded nearby during the war, and the ceilings had all come down. Downstairs, on the left as you went into the hall, were two large reception rooms, separated only by a curtain, which we drew to keep the warmth in the rear one, our sitting room. The front room housed the large table and sideboard Dad had made in Argentina, so it was our dining room, but used only on special occasions. The other front room, on the right of the hall as you came in, was designated the playroom, later to become the study. Behind it was the kitchen. 'This is where we will eat,' Mrs Williams remembers Dad saying as he placed his hand firmly on the kitchen table, which could accommodate six, or seven at a pinch. To the right of the kitchen a couple of steps led down to a passage between us and the neighbours, open but glassed over, which we called the yard. Here was a coal hole, through which every so often coal and coke would be delivered to the cellar below. The cellar was a large area, which housed not only the coal, but initially also Dad's work bench and carpentry things. The windows had an 'X' of brown tape stuck on them to minimise splintering if they were shattered by a bomb blast, and that tape remained in place to the day we sold the house.

The only inside toilet in the house was oddly positioned half way up the stairs. Neither it, nor the bathroom, on the left as you reached the landing, was an original feature of the house. The other toilet, appropriately named 'spiders,' was in the yard. The first floor contained the four bedrooms. The best was in front above the big reception room, with its own little dressing room and basin; this was occupied by Grannie (Mum's mother Nellie Levi) for a while. To its rear, with a fine view of the garden, was Mum and Dad's room, while we children had the smaller rooms on the other side of the landing – Jonathan and Caroline in front, Robin and I behind them. Some rough stairs led up to an attic with a dormer window overlooking the garden and a skylight in the roof.

All the way along the back of the house was a picturesque veranda that caught the afternoon sun. The back garden itself was a fairly standard lawn surrounded by flower beds, with a large but decrepit green house in one corner. There was room for a garage at the side. When we arrived it consisted of an ugly corrugated iron structure. It was in fact an Anderson air raid shelter, but the Lays used the cellar as their shelter and kept their little car in the 'garage', so Mrs Williams told us. The front garden was also fairly standard, with a privet hedge, which Mum hated, along the front wall and down one side.

For me, to be at home was to be on holiday. As a boarding school boy, I was not encumbered by school work when at home. We always had some enjoyable construction work to do: machines and buildings out of Meccano and Minibrix; all manner of models from semi-prepared card; race tracks for our Dinky Toys. Every holiday we would set out and play with Robin's new train, smaller than the large one we had in Temperley.

We were also aeroplane-mad. In Rio we had been excited by the aeroplanes that just seemed to miss the Sugar Loaf Mountain as they came in to land. At Warwick Lodge we were able to observe the growing air traffic into Heathrow from the very beginning. There were few enough flights to make us abandon whatever we were doing (including meal times) to rush out and spot the planes. We made our own model planes from kits bought at Beazley's model shop in Heath Road, Twickenham. I would buy simple gliders that didn't require much putting together. They flew, more or less, in the garden. Robin went in for more complicated structures. Like the earliest flying machines they were made out of wooden struts. Each piece had to be cut out and carefully glued together, then covered with very thin paper, which was stiffened with banana oil, which we appropriately called 'dope'. Mum didn't allow Jonathan and Caroline near us when we were 'doping', saying it was bad for them. Making a model took days, and Robin would not be hurried. The weakest part in the design was the propeller, which was powered by an elastic band running the length of the fuselage. This meant that in flight the models quickly ran out of power as the elastic band unwound and often crash-landed. I vividly remember one occasion when Robin spent even longer than usual on the construction, as I became more and more impatient, having long ago finished my own simple model. Finally the plane was ready for flight, and we solemnly took it out into the garden, where Robin wound it up and launched it. It flew rather well, but, alas, straight into one of the apple trees in the middle of the lawn. The nose section buckled and the plane was pronounced useless. I was beside myself with disappointment and frustration, but Robin calmly picked up the remains of the model and said, 'Never mind, Mart – the fun's in the making. Let's go and buy another one!' So off we went to Beazley's.

In winter time we had the playroom, which we shared with Jonathan and Caroline. That made setting up anything like a model railway difficult, so we tended to do that in the attic, when it wasn't too cold. Mum would say sternly at breakfast, 'Now where are you boys going to play?' On the answer depended which room would be heated and how. In the playroom we could light a coal fire. In the attic we had an electric heater that looked like a modern satellite dish – an element heated up in the centre of a saucer shaped metal disc, ensuring that a fierce heat was projected straight ahead without apparently affecting the temperature of the room as a whole. There was no question in those days of playing in our rooms: there wasn't enough space, and they were too cold. Some of the bedrooms had gas fires, which were turned on as a great concession at getting up time and going to bed time in the coldest winter weather, or when one of us was sick. Life became more comfortable when Dimplex radiators (oil-filled, electric-powered and portable) came on the market.

******

We did not have many visitors. We had few close relations, Dad being an only child and Mum's brother Martin being childless. Martin and his wife Bubbles visited occasionally. These were rather tense occasions, as they were demanding guests with a standard of living well above ours, and Dad would quail as the amply proportioned Bubbles advanced on him to embrace him, 'continental shelf' jutting out alarmingly, sometimes topped with a dangerously spiky ornament. Robin and I visited them from time to time during the holidays, which were also rather quite a strain, as they overfed us with the wrong type of food, which our upbringing taught us we had to eat. Uncle Martin once gave Robin and me a tour of Barker Bros, the family silver factory. It was by turns exciting – we electroplated our own penny coins; dispiriting – I saw an antiquated production line for the first time and the drudgery it involved; and intimidating – we lunched with the entire board. Years later I gathered that the visit was designed in part as an inducement to us (Robin in particular) to join the family firm in due course, but we were not drawn to it.

We were fortunate that Mum's first cousin, Dr Ruth Haes, the daughter of her aunt Dorothy, lived and worked in Twickenham.

She became our family doctor and was joined by her cousin Toppy, back from Australia again, as housekeeper. Ruth died of cancer in 1961, but before that Toppy had moved away to look after Mrs Botha Hawkins, the elderly widow of a Boer War veteran, in a 'Grace and Favour' apartment in Hampton Court (so called because they were made available by the sovereign to deserving citizens for services to crown and country). We quite enjoyed visiting her, nonchalantly walking past the 'No Public Access' signs to her chilly rooms with a beautiful view over a sunken garden.

As children we got along pretty harmoniously, partly because the difference in age (Robin and I three years apart, Jonathan and Caroline two, with a five-year gap in between) meant that we inevitably divided into two pairs. We older boys were rather quiet, the younger children rather excitable by the standards of the time. Robin and I weren't always kind to 'the kids,' and Jonathan once burst into tears at lunch, complaining (no doubt with justification) that 'Robin and Martin are so *beastly* to me!' Robin and I, having explained our behaviour not very satisfactorily, took ourselves off in a huff after lunch ('I don't think we're wanted much here, Mart'), but returned for tea, having played a few mental cricket games and collected enough poplar leaves for our caterpillars.

Our life was very regular. After breakfast Dad would cycle off to work. (One summer's day Mum took us for a boat trip down to Hampton Court, and as we passed by the Lensbury Club we were thrilled to see him coming down the lawn to the riverside to wave to us.) Mid-morning there were elevenses (or 'middles' as we called this ritual) with Mrs Williams. Lunch was the main meal, and high tea, an egg done in some way, for example, around five. Dad must have had his main meal in the office, for when he came home he was pretty quickly absorbed into a game of Mah-jong, or Canasta when that was all the rage. On winter evenings we sat in a large circle around the sitting room fire, the radio usually tuned to the recently established BBC 'Third Programme' (precursor to Radio 3) for the evening's concert, and Mum surrounded by a pile of darning, until we had to brave the cold hall and bedroom, with a bath, not very deep and not very hot for the No 2 (we always shared), as our main comfort.

******

Christmas took up a whole holiday. The moment we returned from school we got down to making decorations. The staple raw material was green and red crêpe paper, which we cut into strips, each strip being joined with paste and made into a link in a long chain. One year we bought some metallic strips, which we hung from various fittings where they were supposed to reflect the light prettily. They were in fact military surplus: they had hung from barrage balloons during the war to confuse enemy radar. As Christmas decorations they were heavy, dull in colour and with unpleasantly sharp edges. I don't remember our having a Christmas tree at all – how would we have transported it home, having no car?

Our celebrations were traditional. We had stockings first thing on Christmas morning, packed with a predictable but exciting assortment of pencils, notebooks and little toys, with a tangerine or apple always filling out the toe section. Then there was church – the long walk to St Stephen's in East Twickenham. Geographically, our local church was All Souls at the Isleworth end of Ailsa Road, but it was too 'high' for us. There was then a seemingly interminable wait for our Christmas meal while Mum roasted the chicken (a luxury in those days of rationing) and various accessories. Finally we would come to the meal, in the dining room. After the chicken we would have Christmas pudding, made by Mum. Like most children I didn't care for it much, but there was excitement there too, as it concealed silver sixpenny pieces, which brought luck. After one or two years we discovered that the sixpenny bits were not silver at all and should not have been brought into contact with things we ate, so we transferred to Australian sixpenny bits and then to some fine little silver ornaments, which were reused, of course.

Mum did her best to set the table out elegantly. Being from a silversmith's family she had some good cutlery, if not pure silver. At one point she even introduced finger bowls so that we could get the stickiness off our fingers after eating crystallised fruit (a great favourite and quite rare). I scorned all the finery in favour of crackers, especially those that contained 'indoor fireworks'. Metal trays would be put out to stop them burning the table cloth, and Dad would put a match to them. They would burn with a coloured flame, unravel into fantastic shapes or give off a little explosion. Quite modest, but for me more worth while than the outdoor variety, which never seemed to justify the extensive preparations they required.

We didn't usually have guests, though initially Grannie would be with us. On one occasion she took us out to a Christmas meal at a restaurant in Richmond, where we all had to be on our best behaviour. On another occasion we had Cousin Ruth after Toppy had gone back to Australia and she was all on her own. That was also hard going: Ruth lacked a sense of fun. After the meal we had presents – items for the train, Dinky Toys, Meccano, Minibrix and the like. Our paternal grandmother was a lavish present giver, but didn't always spend wisely. One Christmas she gave Robin and me enormous battery powered boats that really sailed. But they were far too heavy for their motors, so not much use.

The dreary part came after Christmas: thank you letters, which I made very heavy weather of; taking down the decorations; and the rather empty couple of weeks before we went back to school. Winters could be quite bleak and dirty in those days. This was the era of coal fires. When their smoke was trapped under a layer of cold air fog turned to 'smog'. Washing hung outside would be retrieved covered in soot. The great London smog of December 1952 is estimated to have killed some ten thousand people. Even in better weather there wasn't much to be done outside, but on some Saturday afternoons we went with Dad to a rugger match at Twickenham,

First summer in Warwick Lodge: with Robin,
Jonathan and Caroline on the veranda, August 1948

where Harlequins were the resident team and therefore 'ours'. We walked the long walk down the by-pass to the ground, bought our tickets for two shillings and sixpence (2/6 as we wrote it – cheap, although not as cheap as a strict conversion to today's currency, just 12.5p, would suggest) and found a barrier to lean against in the primitive South Stand. We followed the same procedure for internationals, but we were treated to a drop of rum in our milky coffees before we set off (to ward off the cold), reached the ground a little bit earlier to get a good vantage point and paid some 4/- instead of 2/6. Sometimes the games were exciting, especially if the tries were scored at 'our' end. But the standard was not then what it is now, and games could be very slow-moving as well as being pretty well invisible when play moved to the other end, dusk fell and the players all but disappeared under a cloud of steam and mist.

Easter holidays were enlivened by the Good Housekeeping Exhibition in Earls Court, where we could get a huge variety of free samples, together with brochures and other bits and pieces. Cross & Blackwell, its stand piled high with tins and bottles, once ran a competition to estimate the number of items on display. 'OK, Mart,' said Robin, 'let's count them up.' And so he did – not an easy job as there were mirrors behind, tempting you to double count, as well as pyramids of tins on revolving stands, which meant that you had to fix on one eye-catching product and count until it came round again. But we had time, and Robin had method and patience. We were allowed to submit one entry each. With his usual generosity Robin assigned to me the number he thought most likely to be right, giving himself one number higher. Of course 'my' number was right, and a week or so later, after Robin had returned to Oundle, but I was in bed recovering from chicken pox, a large Cross & Blackwell hamper arrived. It was a moment of intense excitement, even if some bottles of pickle were not our thing at all and were given away to Mrs Williams and others.

In the summer holidays we went out more, and as we grew older we were allowed to ride our bikes further than 'up and down' Ailsa Road. We would cycle to Marble Hill Park for a game of tennis, or even as far as Richmond Park. But it was cricket that dominated our lives. Not so much playing – we were not great players and did no more than set up our little cricket pitch in the back garden. It was rather that everything we did became a game of cricket. Robin even invented a cricket match that could be played as we walked along the by-pass (now the A316) to Richmond and back, using the number plate of each passing vehicle (they were still quite few and far between in those days) to represent a batsman's score, which he of course managed to add up and keep track of in his head.

At some point, after much yearning and counting up of Christmas and birthday present equivalents, we acquired a superior table cricket game called Discbat. The 'bowler' bowled by dropping a small metal ball down a chute, upon which the 'batsman' released a metal disc (hence the name) aiming to drive the ball sweetly past the plastic fielders, all of whom had a little pouch that could 'catch' the ball. This excellently designed game came to dominate our lives, as Robin wove a whole County Championship round it. We doggedly played out matches between our favourite counties, while Robin compiled endless books of statistics. He even made a cunning scoreboard out of wood.

The closest we got to real cricket were excursions to Lord's Cricket Ground, where Middlesex played. It would have been easier and cheaper to watch Surrey playing at the Oval – Vauxhall being just a few stations up from St Margaret's – but we wouldn't hear of it. Dad had always been a Middlesex supporter and so were we. The fact that we actually came to live in the county of Middlesex after the *annus mirabilis* of 1947, when Middlesex had won the county championship, was an added bonus. Besides, our finely tuned class instinct told us that Lord's was more for People Like Us. So to Lord's we went. Our weekday visits followed a regular pattern – Southern Railway from St Margaret's to Waterloo, Bakerloo Line on the tube to St John's Wood, and a good walk from there to the ground. Having arrived before the gates opened we would stand in a queue, then pay our two shillings or so to get in, buy a scorecard for threepence and settle into seats on the upper stand at the nursery end, opposite the pavilion. The scorecard was important: it gave all the necessary information about the teams and the scores from the previous day's play. We (i.e. Robin) would then meticulously fill it in as the day progressed. County Championship matches could be pretty slow-paced, but we never contemplated leaving before the last ball of the day had been bowled, or, if it was raining, until play was officially called off. We looked askance at any of our very occasional guests who did. We scarcely moved from our seats and never bought any refreshments at the ground. Mum made us sandwiches for lunch (or my favourite bacon and egg pie) and a thermos of tea. For me, whatever the state of play, lunch time was the most eagerly anticipated event of the day, with tea a close second.

Another reason for going to Lord's was Dad's membership of the prestigious MCC (Marylebone Cricket Club – I was shocked to discover at some point that the M did not stand for Middlesex, who merely rented Lord's from this amorphous body). So on a

115

Saturday we could sit with him in the members' guest stand, next to the pavilion. It was Dad's dream to have us accepted as members as soon as we were old enough, and he had connections in the shape of Frank and George Mann, father and son and both captains of Middlesex in their time. Apparently Dad's mother had nursed Frank Mann during the First World War. So during the lunch interval, Robin and I would wait sheepishly outside the pavilion, while Dad went in search of one or other of the great men (or any other whom he managed to buttonhole) in order to present us to them. His persistence paid off and we got our membership rather ahead of our turn in the lengthy queue for this privilege. Dad would have liked to bring Mum to cricket matches, but she made it a condition that she should be allowed to bring her knitting, which for all his generosity of spirit Dad couldn't bring himself to accept.

As the cricket season drew to a close there was the Farnborough air show to look forward to. We would go by train on the Friday to avoid the Saturday crowds, Dad presumably taking the day off work. It was an exciting event, which one year ended in tragedy. On Saturday 6th September 1952 the twin-bodied De Havilland DH110 disintegrated in mid-air after breaking the sound barrier. One of its engines ploughed into the crowd, killing thirty people. I was seized with horror as I read about the accident in the paper – we had been there only the previous day watching the same plane doing its display. We continued to go to Farnborough, but I was always nervous. Mum must have been out of her mind with worry, but she didn't betray it to us.

Another summer activity was hunting butterflies. There were more to be found in the garden than you would find nowadays, and we had a fine buddleia tree that attracted them. I went weak at the knees when I caught my first Red Admiral. We would suffocate them in an ether bottle and set them on special boards, though we never got as far as making a display collection. The great prize was the Camberwell Beauty, which I think we never saw, let alone caught. What I really enjoyed about butterfly collecting was getting the kit – nets, setting boards etc, which one ordered by mail (postal order for a modest sum enclosed). We probably got our ether from Swann's the chemists. Like the 'dope' for our model aeroplanes, this was a substance one can hardly imagine two teenagers buying over the counter today. At one point we decided to breed butterflies from caterpillars kept in an old biscuit box with air holes punched out in the lid. We may have got the idea from an article in the first *Eagle* Annual about breeding silkworms. We left the box in our desk when we went back to school. Perhaps we thought we would retrieve the caterpillars as chrysalises in the next holidays. In fact, guided by an increasingly repugnant smell, Mum had to retrieve the rotting caterpillars from the desk and throw the whole lot away.

We tried fishing once. Fishing rods were too expensive, so we bought lines on reels. It was proper fishing tackle, but probably meant to be played out off the end of a boat. Standing at the edge of the river at low tide just below Richmond lock we found it difficult to get the lines out into the water. The experiment was short lived, in any case. A frisky dog jumped up at me, and, panicking, I abandoned my line and ran home crying, Robin following me out of solidarity. I was convinced I had been bitten, though no traces of a bite were found. Nonetheless, it put an end to my fishing enthusiasm and left me with a fear of dogs that lasted for years.

One summer activity that I didn't particularly enjoy was 'Bob-a-job'. This was a Boy Scouts fund raising activity, perhaps the only task I was set from Forres to do at home. It meant hawking my services around neighbours – cutting their grass or doing some cleaning – in exchange for a shilling (a 'bob'), duly entered in my work sheet and handed in next term. I have an uncomfortable feeling that Mum did most of the preparatory work softening up the neighbours, as I was too timid to approach them 'cold'. Most of them gave me twice the amount of money for only a token piece of work, but at Cousin Ruth's house at No 2 Chudleigh Road, under the supervision of Toppy I really earned my bob, since I had to cut the small lawn with nothing more than a large pair of kitchen scissors. Toppy did give me lunch, however, and it was on one of these visits that she introduced me to what she called 'esh p'titers', which I finally understood was Australian for potatoes baked in the hot ash in the grate of the stove. Quite good, except that it was a point of honour in our household to eat the skin as well, which this method made a little gritty.

Robin and I were expected to help in the house and garden, where Mum and Dad were always hard at work at weekends. We mowed the lawns and trimmed the edges, or lent a hand in big clearing jobs, such as the removal of the hated privet hedge along the front wall. Dad did the heavy work on trees and tackled obvious weeds (oxalis was his pet hate), but otherwise revelled in his reputation as a horticultural ignoramus. He loved to tell the story of how he was up on the roof of the neighbour's chicken coop at the end of our garden, clearing the gutter, when the man labouring on the other side asked him, 'Are you the guv or the gardener?' 'Both,' replied Dad, with aplomb.

Creative gardening was entirely Mum's preserve, and she launched herself into it the year we arrived. We children assimilated a lot, but I for one didn't develop a real interest in gardening until I had one of my own. Dad's building projects included the complete reconstruction of the dilapidated greenhouse and many 'crazy-paving' paths, which involved abundant manual labour. I enjoyed some of the concrete mixing process, which required skill and judgement if the water was not to spill all over the place, but after the second or third mix I would tire and go off to play hide and seek with Jonathan and Caroline, justifying it by claiming that I was 'looking after the kids'. There were some jobs I couldn't get out of, however. Pointing was one. This meant gouging out and replacing the crumbling mortar from the brick walls that went along both sides of the garden, a seemingly endless task. A worse task, which we probably did only once, was painting the corrugated iron 'garage' at the side of the house. No position on this dreadful structure – sitting, crouching or kneeling – could be comfortable as we daubed on the sticky green paint under a burning sun. It was a relief when it was taken down as part of a major building project – an extension to the house including an integral garage.

The worst job of all, but one which had a whiff of heroism about it, was to receive the occasional coal delivery. A couple of men from the coal merchant (one of the ubiquitous Gay brothers, who had his shop on the road to Isleworth) would dump the coal by the sack-load at great speed through the manhole in the yard. Robin and I would be down below in the cellar, clad only in our underpants and some old shoes and armed with shovels, desperately trying to stop the coal mounting up and blocking the manhole. If it did, Gay's men would mechanically continue their dumping till coal was all over the yard. Once delivered, the coal had to be shifted into a separate compartment of the cellar, away from the manhole, to make room for a later delivery of coke for the kitchen boiler. At the end of this exercise we would emerge like miners coming up from their shift and make for the bath, shedding as little coal dust on the stairs as we could.

We provided a little bit of help taking Jonathan and Caroline to Edwina House School in the neighbouring St Peter's Road. Later we would occasionally fetch Caroline from St Stephen's Primary School not far away across the by-pass (indeed the family joke was that we knew when classes had finished by the sound of Caroline's voice carrying all the way from the playground). A more daunting task for me, which I probably did only once, was to fetch Caroline from her ballet class, a long walk down the by-pass to the beginning of Kew Road, where a formidable teacher drilled a small class of girls in very small premises. Going in, I found myself faced by a large curtain, from behind which, over the music and stomping feet, came a stentorian voice: 'Who are you and who do you belong to?' Luckily I had been primed and nervously answered both parts of the question. After a few minutes Caroline burst through the curtain and we were on our way, without my ever having glimpsed the class or the owner of the voice.

We were also expected to help with the shopping. Nearly all of it could be done in St Margaret's, whose row of shops leading up to the station we knew intimately. First there was the optician, B. Lloyd Waters. Because of our connection with Curry & Paxton we didn't use his services professionally, but we liked him because he ran an advertisement on Platform 1 of St Margaret's Station featuring a competition every month which Robin and I diligently solved while waiting for our train up to Waterloo. One month we won the little prize he offered, to our great delight.

Further up the road was N. Lyons the cobbler, where we had our shoes soled and heeled. We always called him 'Mr Nylons' and had difficulty remembering his real name if we wanted to refer to him. He had thick glasses and a slightly manic look, which could be quite scary when he told us, as he often did, that as a result of a war wound he had a metal plate fixed in the back of his head. His was a narrow shop, as the shop front was divided into two, and on the other side of the partition was Miss Richardson, who sold sweets. Bull's Eyes, an interesting pyramidal shape with black and white stripes, were my favourite. We had also quite liked Liquorice Allsorts until one day Robin over-indulged and was violently sick.

One shop which bore no interest for us, but where we sometimes had to go as a duty, was F. C. Yates, the butcher. It was a real butcher's shop with great hunks of meat hanging on hooks and two massive wooden counters on either side of the shop, each manned by one of the ruddy-faced Yates brothers, who (in the best Happy Families tradition) themselves looked like large slabs of meat. There was sawdust on the floor and a cunning system of payment whereby they avoided touching money with their blood-stained hands. Having cut and weighed the meat, they wrote down the cost of your purchase on a piece of paper and put it in a little metal container which they then propelled along a wire until it came to a stop with a clang at the cashier's booth at the back of the shop, where we paid. The reason that we boys were reluctant to shop there was simply that we could do nothing except read out Mum's order from a piece of paper – any follow-up questions about a type of cut or an alternative floored us and we felt humiliated. Although both the Mr Yates looked exactly the same to us, we knew that there was a 'nice Mr Yates,' who dealt kindly with our helpless embarrassment, and a 'nasty Mr Yates,' who seemed to revel in it.

A more intriguing shop was Frederick Swann's chemist shop next door. This was strictly a dispensing chemist, with men in white coats mixing substances from rows of bottles on shelves and carefully labelling the result 'the Mixture' or 'the Powder.' For a broader assortment of chemists' goods we went down Crown Road to M. E. Simpson. Robin and I once needed some camphor as fuel for a little model boat we had made and rather nervously asked for it in Swann's without knowing the cost. The assistant took a small piece between finger and thumb and said, making the most of the suspense, 'A piece like this costs … sixpence!' From then on we nicknamed him 'A piece like this'. His lanky colleague we called 'The blade of grass'.

Dad's Mecca was Reynolds, a shop that sold more or less everything for the household. There we would find Mr Reynolds himself ('Young Mr Reynolds' to those who had known his father), his unmarried sister and an assortment of assistants, each of whom had his nickname – Sharp Face, Monkey Face and – on busy Saturday mornings – a man of Oriental appearance whom we called 'the Mongolian'. If we wanted something a little unusual one of these people would disappear down a ladder into the basement and return later triumphantly bearing it. We joked that Reynolds' basement stretched the whole length of the street, and what he couldn't find in his own shop he would simply pick up from someone else's. The whole operation was hugely labour intensive, and as self-service DIY shops boomed it became clear that Reynolds was struggling. In truth you tended to come out of the shop having bought what he had offered rather than what you really wanted to buy. One day we were horrified to find completely strange people serving there: the shop and the name had been sold in great secrecy, so as not to lose custom. But it didn't last long under the new management and eventually became a video hire shop.

My Mecca was next door – Alex R. Toombs, the toy shop that sold everything from Dinky Toys to bicycles. It was there that I bought my first real bicycle with its much coveted three-speed gear, which served me for a good 30 years. Further up the road was Phelps, the used furniture store, which provided Mum and Dad with quality items at reasonable prices, a greengrocer who delivered, and, finally Osmond's the grocers. Osmonds was one of three grocers (Home & Colonial and Hornby & Clarke being the others). It was the smallest, but maybe we chose them because they delivered. Every week Mum (or Robin or I in holiday time) would take an order book to the back of the shop and simply hand it over, together with our ration books. They would deliver the order later in the day, noting which items were not in stock or where they had provided substitutes. Not having a car, we would have had enormous difficulty bringing back all the greengroceries and groceries for a family of six on foot. So in a way our shopping for staples anticipated today's on-line shopping, except that we placed our order not on line but on foot. Bread we got from J. Hare, the baker, down Crown Road.

We used Richmond rather seldom. We weren't great walkers, and getting the 37 bus was a tiresome business. For bigger shopping expeditions we went to Kingston and specifically Bentalls, where Mum had an account. Bentalls was exciting. From time to time chimes (sounding just like today's Friedland chimes which so many people have as a front door bell) would ring out, and a well modulated voice would announce 'Bentalls calling!' before announcing the latest bargains. Bills and receipts would be shot around the store in vacuum pipes with a powerful whooshing sound. It was in Bentalls that we would buy our shoes from a Scottish sales assistant, who confused us by recommending each and every shoe as 'a vurry gid shuu'.

******

My interest in events outside my little world developed only gradually. The London Olympics of 1948 passed me by completely, although some of the athletes were billeted nearby in Richmond Park. But the Festival of Britain in 1951 loomed large. It was said that our near neighbour, Mrs Fidler, had won the competition to name the needle-like spire that was one of the landmarks of the Festival as the Skylon (with its 'nylon' and 'pylon' modern technology associations). Robin and I spent a day there, the Festival (bomb) site being just a step away from Waterloo Station. Apart from the Skylon, the main attraction was the Dome of Discovery (or the Dome of Dish-covery, as a cartoon in Punch wittily had it). It was divided into two halves, the one dealing with people and the other with things, and since we knew we would not have time to do both we followed Robin's choice – things. I recall being a bit disappointed. My real disappointment, however, was learning that everything apart from the Festival Hall was to be taken down and thrown away after the Festival was over. We were a thrifty family, and destroying something so recently created seemed a huge waste of money. With a surer instinct I also regretted the destruction of the venerable shot tower on the site, which today would have been a good tourist attraction.

The other major event of the early fifties was the Coronation of Queen Elizabeth II on 3rd June 1953. Oundle closed down for a few days, and we were sent home. Robin and I watched the procession from a vantage point at the edge of Hyde Park. We chose it because it was on high ground rather than close to the route. It was not crowded, and we would have got just as good a position had we arrived shortly before the procession rather than at five or six in the morning as we did. As we arrived the morning papers were trumpeting the ascent of Everest by Hillary and Tensing, so patriotic fervour was in the air. However, it rained ceaselessly all day and we didn't see all that much. As the Queen's closed carriage passed, a kind gentleman behind me allowed me to stand on his toes so that I could see a little bit more But for me, as for many others, the sight of the day was the big, black and beaming Queen of Tonga, soaked to the skin in her open carriage, and loving it. Equally memorable in our family annals was Robin's managing the entire day without going to the lavatory. Our family had split up for the occasion. Dad had earlier joined the Special Constabulary with the express intention of policing such occasions (he had already done the late King's funeral and was to do Churchill's), so he had been on duty since early morning. Mum and Caroline watched the event on a new-fangled projecting television screen set up in the vestry of St Stephen's church, while Jonathan did the same at Forres.

'Old' Commonwealth citizens came over in droves for the event, among them Micky Cowper – Toppy's niece and our fourth cousin – and her friend Mavis Wheeler from Australia. They stayed with us in the intervals between their hitch-hiking tours until Micky left in September, after which Mavis stayed on with us for another three years – fitting her sleeping arrangements around our absences at school. Mavis fitted our family perfectly – hard-working, uncomplicated and able not only to tolerate endless teasing about her funny accent and vocabulary ('washer' for 'flannel' and so on), but give her own back in good measure, chiefly on the lines of everything in Australia being *bigger*. She had a variety of secretarial jobs in the locality, to which she would go every morning clutching a sandwich or two made of anything (but *anything*, including gravy) left over from the day before.

It was at Mavis's initiative that she and I made an epic cycle trip to France in 1955, wobbling our way around the *Arc de*

Triomphe through the thick of Parisian traffic before meandering down the Loire valley looking at *châteaux* and staying at youth hostels. It was noble of Mavis, in her mid-thirties, to take on this gawky eighteen-year old, and we got on remarkably well together despite heat, and rain on the last few days of our journey.

******

Ailsa Road was a middle class road. More precisely, an upper middle class road. Our immediate neighbour on the left at No 15 was General George Tuck of the Royal Engineers, who with his wife Nel had three boys – twin sons George (Tubby) and Brian, of whom one was in the army, and Mitchell, who was about Robin's age and also went into the army. They had a Rolls Royce and a gardener, and Mum and Dad found them a little patronising. Hence Dad, not entirely in jest, would define our status as the writer George Orwell had described his – 'lower-upper middle class', that is, 'upper-middle class without money'. But the Tucks were kind and once took Robin and me to a musical in town, before which they treated us to a meal at the Trocadero in Piccadilly. It was a buffet where you just piled up your plate. Not being used to such freedom of choice I overdid it and, alas, was sick in the Rolls Royce on the way home. When the Tucks retired to Wiltshire, their place was taken by Victor and Biddy Pike, with whom Mum and Dad had much warmer relations. He was Chaplain General to the Armed Forces, a rugby-playing Irishman of massive proportions with a schoolboy sense of humour. Victor later became Suffragan Bishop of Sherborne, with a house in the close of Salisbury Cathedral, a perfect move, as it gave Mum and Dad the opportunity to visit them when visiting Caroline at Godolphin School near Salisbury.

On the other side of us at No 11 were the Lines, an elderly couple who soon gave way to Mrs Ure, a rich Scottish widow, and her companion, Miss Mackenzie (it was common at the time for a widow to have someone, usually a single lady, who would keep her company in return for board and lodging). Mrs Ure was a little overpowering and would screech 'Maaat'n!' at me through the scraggy privet hedge (of which more below) between our front gardens. One memorable evening she invited Robin and me to supper and a game of Mah-jong, having learnt that this was one of our favourite pastimes. We were getting into an embarrassing situation, as her concept of the rules had little in common with ours, but events were soon overtaken by the dramatic appearance of Miss Mackenzie, ghostly white, who asked in a shaking voice, 'Have you been showing the boys your jewels?' Obviously not, so Mrs Ure rushed upstairs, only to return immediately, crying, 'Ach, me jewels, me opals, all gone!' She had been burgled as we played, by someone shinning up the drain-pipe. We rushed home to fetch Dad, for whom Mrs Ure poured a stiff whisky, only to snatch it back at the last moment to drink it herself, to Dad's consternation. She had had decorators in the house, so it looked as though the burglar had had a tip off. For a while we felt a bit vulnerable – our two houses were identical in construction – but it wore off.

Whisky also figured across the road at No 24, inhabited by another rich widow, Mrs Rabbidge, and her companion, another Scot, Miss Fraser. Mrs Rabbidge sat in her first floor sitting room, from where she commanded a view of all of our comings and goings. The Tucks hinted that she appreciated visitors, so Dad, sometimes accompanied by one of us, would go from time to time for a whisky before supper. Despite the inducement he didn't much enjoy the occasion as conversation was limited. Mrs R would always start with a snort of 'Dreadful, isn't it?' She would be referring to whatever the scare headline was in the *Evening Standard*, which she had delivered to her door. Dad would squint at the paper lying on the coffee table and try to deduce what 'it' was before muttering some mollifying remark. Miss Fraser would complain about the East wind, which always seemed to attack her, even when there was a raging gale from the West. 'There's a little bit of East in it as well,' she would maintain.

Next door to Mrs Ure at No 9 were the Roundells, with a young family like ours, but I got the impression that Mum and Dad found them a bit too rich and dashing. In any case we didn't know them well. Opposite them, at No 8, were the Mostyns – Captain Thomas, his wife Hilda and three daughters. They also had a son, an army officer, who was killed in the fighting during the handover of the British Mandate in Palestine around 1948. I was embarrassed when we went to offer condolences, as I was completely out of my depth, emotionally and politically. The boy had been killed by

Family group: in Warwick Lodge garden,
September 1951

Israelis, whom I had understood we were trying to help. The Mostyn girls once invited Robin to a tennis party, which caused a kerfuffle in our household, as he had none of the right equipment or clothes. We were convinced they were all in love with him, as was Ann Bidmead, the beautiful daughter of a widower at No 16. She went into acting, where she used her more romantic first name, Sylvia, and played small parts in films and TV in the 1960s.

I was attracted more to the Isleworth end of the road, where the houses were not so grand, but where two families had television sets: Colonel (Walter) Crook and his sister Ruth, at whose house (No 40) I watched my first ever TV programme, a rather disappointing studio play about the war, with none of the exciting action you got from a real film; and the Robinsons at No 27, whose daughter Heather would invite us, including Jonathan and Caroline, to watch

Muffin the Mule on Children's TV. I don't think my parents so much as dreamt of indulging in the luxury of a television of our own.

******

I find it sad to record that my grandparents figured largely as a burden and a worry. We had missed what might have been the best years with them by our absence in South America during the war. My maternal grandfather, Clive Levi, whom I am said to take after, had died in 1939. Memories of our early years in Warwick Lodge are interwoven with memories of the final years of the three remaining grandparents, all of whom died between 1951 and 1955. Mum and Dad were both chronic worriers – to the extent that I came to assume that worrying was a badge of adulthood – and the emotional and practical complications surrounding their parents' ageing and death caused them as much worry as anything.

Grannie (Mum's mother Nellie, Clive's widow) moved down with us from Sutton Coldfield and occupied the main front room with its little dressing room. She would appear at meal times, a distant, baleful figure. She was in the early stages of dementia, and it must have been harrowing for my mother to watch her deteriorate. I resented her presence as distracting my parents' attention from the important things in life, namely me and my concerns. I didn't realise at the time that they too were resentful, as Uncle Martin and Auntie Bubbles, with a large house in Edgbaston and plenty of money, were really better equipped to look after her. At some point Grannie was shipped off to a nursing home in Bournemouth, perhaps to be near her younger brother Noel and his son James, who with his wife Frankie figures in my Forres chapter. She returned to Wyke House, a mental nursing home in Syon Lane, Isleworth, where she died in 1951 after a fall. I was at Oundle and wrote a perfunctory letter of condolence to Mum, but felt relieved, as I was sure she did. Only a few years later, when Caroline said, 'The only time I have seen Mummy cry was when Grannie died,' did I begin to realise that emotions were a little more complex than that.

Dad's parents, Colin and Winifred, Grandpa and Grandma to us, had long been separated, though they never divorced. Grandma lived in Chislehurst with Brigadier George Sutton, who was politely known as her 'lodger'. Grandpa – the old sea dog who never put anything in a cupboard but always stowed it in a locker – lived in a modest bed-sit in Clapham. He had gone to sea at 14 and had risen to be a Captain in the Merchant Navy, but had never made much money. Grandpa came for the occasional Sunday lunch, and I can still see him in my mind's eye, then in his eighties, turning slowly and deliberately into our front garden after walking from the station. After lunch he would have a game of chess with Dad before wending his way slowly back. Dad said that in the old days his father would win the chess, then they were even, and now he could beat his father. I was fascinated by one of Grandpa's fingers, the tip of which had got caught in the rigging somewhere and been amputated. He had a number of hobbies that kept him going, principally Esperanto – an idealistic attempt to create a universal second language that would further international peace and understanding. He always wore his Esperanto badge.

One day Mum and Dad got a telephone call that made them even more worried than usual: 'Grandpa's had a stroke.' It was the first time I had heard the word in the medical context and could see it was serious. After some time in hospital Grandpa ended up in a nursing home in Feltham. We visited him there – by bicycle, a procession of us wending our way through the back streets. Grandpa seemed quite contented: he didn't ask for much by way of creature comforts. He had lost the use of one hand. This made lighting his pipe difficult, but he had devised a way, gripping the matchbox between his knees. He had also made friends with a former editor of the *Surrey Comet*. We had a slightly surreal conversation about current affairs, in which Grandpa was convinced that a naval incident we were discussing involved sailing ships, while his companion thought that the Comet – Britain's most advanced jet air liner, which had crashed – was his former newspaper. In 1954 Grandpa went into West Middlesex Hospital where, in a rare gesture of defiance, he refused to do therapeutic basket making and died.

Grandma was fourteen years younger than Grandpa, so not yet seventy when we came to Warwick Lodge. Although relations between her and my mother (who had 'stolen' her beloved son) were cool, she had provided valuable practical help as a staging post between Sutton Coldfield and Forres. She would visit every so often with George Sutton, with whom we had cordial relations. He was every bit the military man, with bristling moustache and a parade ground shine on his shoes. He told me the secret: 'Never use a brush on them, my boy!' But I remember better Robin's and my visits to Grandma in Chislehurst. They were fairly stilted occasions, as she didn't have a light touch with children, but I treasured them, as more often than not she would give us a tiny porcelain dog from her collection (she had a real lap dog too), which I would use as a 'lucky' – a sort of charm – for our Mah-jong games. On one occasion Grandpa came down from Clapham to join us for supper, so we were able to witness the curious *ménage à trois* that they operated. Unfortunately, getting up from supper Grandpa knocked over and broke a standard lamp, for which he got an earful from Grandma, despite apologising profusely. The following day he took us to a conjuring show somewhere in south London by Jasper Maskelyne, then a great name as a magician. I was a bit disappointed, partly because Maskelyne himself appeared only halfway through, but also because Grandpa was so obviously downcast by his misadventure the previous evening. He asked us to apologise once again on his behalf when we got back to Chislehurst.

Grandma developed Parkinson's disease and went downhill rapidly. I paid two dispiriting visits to her, though I am not sure in which order they came. One was with Mum to a hospital near to Grandma's home. We went into a large ward, where I could see no sign of Grandma until to my horror it was revealed that a pathetic and apparently lifeless bundle in a bed in the corner was indeed her. The other was an even more harrowing visit with Dad to the Nightingale Nursing Home in Strafford Road, Twickenham. Dad had carefully prepared crossword puzzles from *The Times* as occupational therapy by pasting a number of competitions and the solutions together on single pieces of card. 'So she can still do the crossword!' I suggested brightly. 'I'm afraid not, Martin,' replied Dad with a catch in his voice, 'She just copies the words from the solutions to the blank spaces in the competition, and she can't manage much of that.' But on this occasion there was no opportunity to introduce the puzzles. As we approached we could hear Grandma screaming abuse at the staff – she maintained that they were trying to drag her out of bed and kill her. Dad vainly attempted to mollify his mother, but we had to leave with her cries, 'You hate me, Carroll, you hate me!' ringing in our ears. Seldom did I see my father so downcast. Some time after that Grandma too was transferred to Wyke House, where she died in 1955, only a year after Grandpa.

That left Great Aunt Ruth, Grandma's older sister, with whom we had spent the day in the family home off Clapham Common just before our departure to Argentina at the beginning of the war. I never really knew her. In 1957 she too died in Wyke House, widowed and childless, so Dad was next of kin. My impression is that Ruth left him a tidy inheritance, which along with Grandma's helped to keep the funds for education flowing. But

Grandma's will was disputed. Some time after her death Dad took Robin and me aside to explain her relationship with George Sutton. 'When I was born,' he said, 'my parents took one look at me and separated.' I well remember this phrase. It didn't seem out of the ordinary at the time, but I now realise Dad was blaming himself for the breakdown of his parents' marriage. We knew about the separation, of course, but Dad wanted to explain delicately that George Sutton had been rather more than a 'lodger', that he was laying claim to part of Grandma's estate, and that Dad was taking him to court. There was a possibility – albeit remote – that the case might get into the press and Dad wanted us to be forewarned. In the event Dad won his case without any publicity, and George Sutton was referred to ever after in the family as 'the defendant'.

******

We children had the usual childhood illnesses, but it was Mum and Dad who at different times were seriously ill. In December 1953 we came home for the Christmas holidays to find Mum just out of hospital after an operation. 'They took out a lump from under her arm,' I was told. In fact she had breast cancer and had had a mastectomy, but in those days it was not spoken about openly. I found it hard to accept that she really wasn't up to doing all the things she always did. In fact she was quite weak, came down from her bedroom for a couple of hours on Christmas Day and then went back to bed. Luckily for us, Dad and Mavis, who made up in organisational skills what they lacked in experience, took over. Dad made up an incredibly clever grid with all our names down the side and across the top to ensure that everyone gave everyone a present.

> But why is there a diagonal line going through the middle, Daddy?
> Well, you don't need to give *yourself* a present, do you, Martin?
> Ah!

Mavis took two months off work to mind the family. She tackled the Christmas lunch bravely, falling behind on the timing a bit, but otherwise coping. I suppose we children did a bit more than usual, although the fact is that in the holidays I was very much in consumer mode and didn't do any more than was specifically demanded of me. in any case, things pretty quickly got back to normal.

Dad's health was generally robust, so it was a shock when a few years later he had his first epileptic seizure. One evening during the holidays Dad was in his bedroom sorting things out before going off on a business trip to Holland the next day. Caroline and Jonathan were asleep and Robin and I preparing for bed when there was a thump on the floor. Mum rushed into the bedroom and immediately out again to ring Cousin Ruth, who came like a shot and ordered an ambulance. Dad was whisked off to West Middlesex Hospital, possibly with Mum in the ambulance, while Robin was left in charge of the rest of us. I was transfixed with fear until it became apparent that Dad was neither dead nor about to die. After a few days he was transferred to the Middlesex Hospital in London where he had a brain scan. It transpired that he had had peculiar symptoms – his pastimes of cricket and music had on occasion actually taken over in his head at work, so for minutes at a time he no longer knew where he actually was. He was ordered to rest, which was frustrating as he felt perfectly well once he had come to. His boss tended to ring up to find out how he was, which added to the stress, as Dad, ultra-conscientious, interpreted the calls as hints that he was malingering. One evening, when we had all planned to go to a firework display at the Twickenham Rugby Ground, I volunteered to stay behind to look after Dad. I actually sat beside him in his bedroom, an indication of how nervous we all were. Dad was lying down, and suddenly the book he was reading fell on his face. My heart missed several beats, but Dad raised the book again and grinned as if it had been a joke. I think he had just fallen asleep, but didn't want to admit it. He had been put on various pills, which robbed him of his energy.

At some point he must have come off the Benzedrine, as I think it was, and then he had his second seizure. This time it was during a summer weekend in daylight and therefore not so frightening. We had just started a major project, replacing the scraggy privet hedge between us and Mrs Ure with a new fence. Only a few bits of privet had been pulled out when suddenly Dad was flat on the ground, with his head in Mrs Ure's garden and his feet in ours. This time the reaction was less panicky, and Cousin Ruth delayed getting the ambulance until it was established that Dad would be taken directly to Middlesex Hospital. I don't remember Dad displaying any of the classic signs of epilepsy, foaming at the mouth or thrashing around with his feet, but in any case I was quickly despatched to St Margaret's Station with a mission to turn back our expected lunch guest, an Oundle friend of Robin's. I met him coming up the stairs, smiling at me thinking he had been given an escort, but having breathlessly explained our predicament I despatched him down the other set of stairs, which he accepted with good grace.

Dad being *hors de combat* had a major effect on the rest of the summer holiday. The fence we were dealing with was Mrs Ure's, not ours. Mum and Dad had long chafed at the awful privet and the access it gave the somewhat overbearing Mrs Ure to our private life. But they knew she was more or less indifferent to it. So Dad had delicately negotiated an agreement under which she paid for a new fence and Dad was to put it up. Now Dad was out of action Robin was promoted from builder's mate to builder and I from mate's mate (which meant that in practice I could do what I liked) to real mate in a job that couldn't physically be done by one person. All plans for leisurely days at Lord's went by the board as we had a deadline – the start of the school term. With Dad supervising us occasionally from the front bedroom window (the nearest he was allowed to approach so that he wouldn't get stressed), Robin worked away methodically, measuring and digging, while I mixed the concrete and held posts for him to set in it, increasingly impatient with his insistence that they should be absolutely vertical. We did finish the fence on time and rewarded ourselves with just one day at Lord's. Never have I enjoyed a day's cricket more. That was Dad's last major seizure, but he was occasionally stopped in his tracks for a few seconds, right into his old age. The fence stood proudly erect for the next fifty years.

******

These dramas behind us, life at Warwick Lodge resumed its normal rhythm. As time went by I became a stroppy, if not rebellious teenager. I would always do the tasks asked of me, but on occasion I would choose not to go on family walks to Kew, preferring to lounge at home listening to opera on Dad's new long playing records. And as Oundle and later the Navy and University became the centre of my life, Warwick Lodge was the place I went back to in order to relax. But it was still home.

Memories of Childhood

Six

Oundle: Childhood
Draws to a Close

' You see, Mart, in the prep-room there are two invisible lines between three tables. When you first arrive you will be on the bottom table and won't be allowed to cross the first line. When you move up to the middle table, you'll be able to cross the first line, but not the second one.'

So Robin confided to me out of the blue as we set out from Warwick Lodge to walk to the shops one day in the summer of 1951, shortly before I was due to start at Oundle.

'There's also an invisible line across the Market Place, and as a new boy you can't cross it – you have to go round through the churchyard to get to the Great Hall and the Cloisters. And in your first term you must carry your books with a straight arm and have all three buttons of your coat done up.'

And so on. Robin was preparing me for the ritual humiliation that was visited on 'new ticks' at Oundle – being bawled at by senior boys for failing to observe informal rules that they could not possibly be expected to know. Hence Robin's conspiratorial tone – he was giving me privileged information that I was supposed to learn the hard way.

I had been to Oundle once before, in June 1951, for the scholarship exam. This was the occasion when I had a spat with my Forres Headmaster Mr Chadwick over what combination of jacket and trousers it was appropriate for me to wear. Thanks to my breaking the journey at home I was able to set off by train for Oundle wearing what I wanted – Forres blazer and grey flannel trousers – and therefore in high spirits. That didn't last, as I missed my Oundle connection at Peterborough, having been directed to the wrong platform. Luckily for me another wretched would-be scholar, Swallow by name, had also been misdirected and was forlornly waiting further down the platform. We made common cause and thanks to his initiative in phoning the school we ended up taking a bus to Kettering, where we were picked up by one of the masters in his car. All this must have taken quite a time, because the other scholarship boys were already sound asleep in a guest dormitory in the 'Tuck Shop' by the time we arrived. We were packed off to bed with a mug of cocoa.

Neither of us got a scholarship. Graham Stainforth, the Headmaster, sent the list of winners to Mum and Dad with a note saying,

I'm sorry Martin did not get anything. He did creditably, but was just below the line.

A few days later Mum wrote to her brother Martin,

Martin has been very unlucky, he passed the qualifying exam for the Oundle schol. & went up there last Mon. to take the next part but has failed to get a scholarship. We were told that his marks were actually very little below Robin's but it was a very strong year. Robin is doing outstandingly well & we feel very proud of him.

My recollection is that I performed miserably, but perhaps I am just thinking of the Greek paper, in which I could barely put pen to paper. I was probably less concerned than Mum and Dad, who could have done with the bursary that went with the scholarship.

******

In those days there were some six hundred and sixty boys at Oundle, but my world was Bramston House, with a mere fifty one. Nine of us were new in the Michaelmas Term of 1951. We were never a closely knit group and soon developed along our different academic, sporting and social lines. I have only kept in touch with a couple of them. But I can picture us all as clearly as yesterday, occupying the bottom end of the bottom table of the dining room. We were always ranked in the same order of seniority, which I think just reflected our age. First on the list was John Clark, with an impeccable pedigree in a House that prized the dynastic tradition. Not only had his father been in Bramston, but so had his uncle, while his cousin Nicholas Herbert was a senior boy in the House and would in due course succeed his father to the hereditary title of Lord Hemingford. Clark was set for quick advancement up the ladder towards House and School prefect, conveniently becoming Head of School in time for the Queen Mother's visit on the School's 400th anniversary in 1956. Neither his appearance nor his personality matched up to this star billing. Gauche and not very bright, he was known affectionately as 'Gob' for his tendency to waffle.

Clark and I were not close friends, but he once invited me up to his grand, castellated house in Haltwhistle, Northumberland, for a week in the summer over my birthday, 12th August. Up there, it was known as the 'Glorious Twelfth', the opening of the grouse shooting season, and a major date in the local calendar. Clark senior, a rather grand estate agent, arranged for me to be invited to the shoot. 'He shoots with a four-ten [a junior shotgun],' I heard him say over the phone. We tramped over the moors, and happily I never hit anything, or anybody. I aimed for a snipe, the barrel of my gun weaving patterns in the air as I tried to follow the bird's flight, until a kindly beater told me that was no way to shoot: 'You point your gun in the general direction of the bird, say "that bird is mine", and shoot.' We had a sandwich lunch, the beaters on one side of the car, the gentlefolk on the other. That was the beginning and end of my career as a shot, apart from potting at rabbits with John from the Clarks' sitting room. I may or may not have hit some, but I was grateful to John for being willing to finish off the wounded by breaking their necks. I was as much of a dud with the rod as with the gun when we fished in the grounds of Alnwick Castle – despite (or perhaps because of) it being impressed on me that this was a rare privilege. The family made much of me on my birthday, and I fell in love with two of John's older sisters simultaneously.

Second in the pecking order was Francis John French, a timid boy who we knew had no father and showed the effect of being brought up by his mother. I rather despised his effeminate

147

manner and was disconcerted when after puberty he quickly overtook me in height and weight. In contrast to French, Christopher Morgan had lost his mother, and the effect of a father's upbringing showed in his abrupt manner. He was a gifted pianist who had won a scholarship partly on that account. I came between French and Morgan, with a pedigree second only to Clark's – an old Bramstonian father and an elder brother in the House. Like them I was 'Nick'. Thanks to Robin's coaching I knew how to avoid the pitfalls and also gained status by 'fagging' for Nicholas Herbert, who was not only a great sportsman and in line for a peerage, but a thoroughly nice person. Fagging meant acting as servant or batman for a House prefect. It was another traditional device to imbue new arrivals with a sense of deference towards their seniors and was by then something of a relic. I vaguely recall cleaning Herbert's shoes and taking him his 'slabbers' (of which more below) for tea, but nothing else. In character I was a swot – studious, but not clever enough to carry it off lightly. I spent hours studying the Blue Book – a pocket-sized termly publication listing all the boys and staff in the School categorised by House and Form – thus marking myself out from an early age as one of life's observers rather than players. Here too I can detect the germ of my later enthusiasm for Kremlinology.

At the end of list came David McFetrich, who was to become my brother-in-law. We called him 'Jeremy', but this was a nickname and had to be pronounced in a special way – *Djie*remy – to get the right effect. It was given to him by a senior boy who claimed that McFetrich was as small as his pet mouse of that name. He was indeed small enough to be a sort of House mascot for a time, with a pronounced (to our ears) Geordie accent adding to his charm. He and I worked our way up the House in quite close contact, with Jeremy in my last term a valued co-editor on the House magazine. He once invited me to stay with him in Sunderland to experience a Northern New Year. In those days New Year celebrations were scarcely known in my part of England, and New Year's Day was just another working day. This visit was in many ways as exotic as that to John Clark's 'castle'. The McFetrich family was the same size as ours, except that the children were all boys, but the culture was different. David's father like mine was no great hand in the kitchen, but whereas mine did as much as he was allowed to do, I had the impression that David's father's status would have been compromised by too close an involvement in domestic arrangements. He was at his best in 'first footing', a Scottish/North of England tradition according to which the first person to cross the threshold of a home after midnight on New Year's Eve would determine the homeowner's luck for the New Year. The ideal visitor should be a man with a dark complexion offering whisky, coal, cakes and a coin, and McFetrich senior was much in demand for this role in his large family. So New Year's Eve was a big celebration in which we wended our way from house to house giving (and of course receiving) goodies. The other big event was to be a launch –

David's father was a shipbuilder – but this, alas, didn't happen, either because of a strike or because of weather conditions.

My more intense friendships were made in due course with boys with whom I had some particular interest in common: Ian Gunn Clarke, with whom I shared a passion for athletics, and who died young in a mountaineering accident; and John Corps, my closest friend towards the end of my time at Bramston, a year or so younger than me, with whom I launched into the study of Russian.

******

Bramston itself was made up of three houses in a terrace facing Oundle Market Place. The handsome main building was the Housemaster's residence. At the back it gave on to an impressive lawn, on which only staff and House prefects could walk, and below that the paddock, open to all. The other two houses were rabbit warrens containing studies, the matron's and the House tutor's rooms, with connections at odd levels between them. My initial home, the prep-room, stretched out from the back of the middle building and overlooked the lawn. It must have been a stable or outhouse originally. From the prep-room we could get into a changing room and upstairs to dormitories under cover, but for every other destination, including the 'bogs' (lavatories) we had to go outside. We were perversely proud of our primitive habitat, rivalled only by New House, at the other end of the main street, and we despised the comforts enjoyed in other Houses, especially St Anthony, the rich boys' House, which boasted central heating.

Much of our activity in the House was centred on eating – greasy bacon and fried bread for breakfast, casseroles with over-boiled greens, followed by a variety of 'stodge' (i.e. suet puddings) for lunch, and something a bit lighter for supper. To this we added doughnuts in the Cloisters at School break time and 'slabbers' in the House at tea time – large hunks of white bread, with a mountain of butter and cold milk to go with them, all laid out on a marble slab (hence the name) at a strategic crossroads between studies, a locker room and the great outdoors. Clutching our portion, we would run back to the prep-room, where we made this unappetising fare palatable by heating it up on primus stoves. The fire risk must have been considerable, but I don't remember any mishaps. At one point I acquired an ingenious device to make a toasted baked bean sandwich. It looked like a pair of bellows, but where the air box would have been there were two fitting metal saucers. They would enclose a couple of slabbers filled with baked beans. Thrust the device into the fire, and in due course you pulled out a crispy brown toasted sandwich, to be washed down with milky hot chocolate – bliss. Despite our diet I don't remember any boy being particularly fat, let alone obese. We took a lot of exercise. As well as a heavy programme of sports we walked everywhere, which meant crossing the town several times in the day. Until my last year, when I made two car trips with members of staff, I did not use any wheeled transport from the moment I got off the train at the beginning of term until the moment I got on it again at the end.

******

With nearly as many boys as in Forres, Bramston was a whole world for me. At Forres we did everything in gaggles, but the emphasis was on developing our individual personalities – *All Things Keenly*. At Oundle, and particularly in Bramston, we were already deemed to be individuals, and sufficiently motivated ones at that; the emphasis was on blending our separate personalities into something beyond ourselves. The watchword was Spirit – Team Spirit, House Spirit, School Spirit. Bramston had the reputation in the School of being somewhat effete: we were lackadaisical, always late, did a lot of music and had a poetry club. Shortly after I arrived, however, Bramston achieved the unthinkable – it almost won the School rugby cup, falling gloriously in the final. House Spirit had never been higher.

The man most responsible for this pleasant state of affairs was Dudley S. Heesom, Bramston's long-serving Housemaster. Some thirteen years previously he had taken over from 'Bufty' Nightingale, who had been Dad's Housemaster, and with whose widow we Nicholson boys would have Sunday tea once a term. I got the impression when I arrived that Mr Heesom was not particularly well-regarded in the School as a whole. He was known as 'Drip' – a wet Housemaster in charge of a wet House. In Bramston he was

Dressed for the Coronation:
Bramston House, Oundle, June 1953

viewed with affection – 'Sir' to his face, but among ourselves 'Heezom' or just 'Dudley'. He was a shambling figure, with his head cocked on one side (the story was that he only had the sight of one eye) and the paunch of an ex-rower whose stomach muscles had gone soft. He was known for his acute mind, and it was said that he could easily have been an Oxford don. For us junior boys this quality translated into rambling soliloquies delivered in the prep-room before bedtime in a querulous, high-pitched voice that we all learnt to imitate. Oddly enough he had a passionate interest in boxing, but he himself seemed utterly gentle. True, he had a collection of canes in his study that he occasionally used (not on me), but his aim was so poor that the main danger was being painfully clipped around the ankles. Dudley was married to Betty, an artist with a love of bright colours, who decorated their house with gaudy wallpapers and after retirement every summer took her husband off to a house in sunny Spain. They had two girls and a boy, who were kept at arms length from us.

I did a term or so in Dudley's European history class, which was enjoyable, not least because he begged us not to take too many notes. Of Empress Irene of Byzantium he enjoined us to note simply 'eyes of son', meaning that she had gouged out her son's eyes. 'That's enough to characterise her.' My very neat notebook is testimony to his careful teaching. Dudley had a famous idiosyncrasy: his lessons were extended monologues, in which he had a tendency to repeat himself, so he encouraged us, rather than look bored when he started on a story he had already told, silently to take the ink pots out of our desks and put them on top. As soon as he saw the pots Dudley would change tack without a pause.

For me Dudley was an avuncular figure, not distant, but not close either. He had the knack of making me feel I was doing well even when I wasn't. I was once on the way to making a fearful mess of the House play I was supposed to be producing at the end of the Michaelmas term. I hadn't really known how to go about it, had failed to find a suitable play, had decided to write one myself (a black comedy involving Hitler and Stalin), and had scarcely finished writing, let alone assembled a cast, with a week or so to go. Providence intervened, as it had once at Forres, in the shape of a flu epidemic that sent us all packing off home a week early, and the House play was abandoned. But Dudley took the trouble to commend my efforts so far. Did he know how far off target I was? That remained a mystery.

The only occasion on which I was upset by Dudley was at the beginning of one term when I arrived back at School with a few chicken pox scabs still adhering to my skin. They were discovered by Dr Spurrell, the School doctor, as he did his regular (and embarrassing) test on all the boys for signs of *tinea* (a fungal infection akin to athlete's foot) under the arms and in the groin. I was summarily packed off to the sanatorium in a taxi after an unpleasant interrogation by Dudley: 'How many other boys have you infected?' In vain did I argue that our well-informed GP (Cousin Ruth) knew that it was no longer necessary to assume that the infectious stage lasted till the last scab had dropped off. I spent a few days in 'solitary' in the san composing angry letters to *The Times* (the only form of public protest I knew) on the backwardness of schools that didn't keep up with the latest medical research. But I was flattered by a visit from Mr Stainforth, the Headmaster, who by happy coincidence found me genuinely absorbed in my French set book.

I think Dudley's main strength was that he treated us, if not as adults, then as boys who could be trusted in general to know what was best for them and get on with their lives without interference.

One episode remains particularly vivid in my memory. Deep in the bowels of the Housemaster's house was the kitchen with a cook and a couple of 'skivvies', middle-aged local women whom we rarely saw and in our arrogant way took no notice of when we did see them. Then, early one summer term, there emerged from the depths two radiant young blondes. The House was in ferment. Normal activities gave way to endless reports of sightings of these divine creatures, while the more forward boys competed with tales of what they might do with them or (some of the more imaginative hinted) might already have done. When matters had reached fever pitch Dudley took action. At the end of his evening monologue he said, as if in passing, 'Some of you …er … may have noticed …er … that we have two new girls working in the kitchen [sniggers]. They are students from Denmark. Do please make yourselves known to them; pass the time of day with them; invite them to your studies for tea. They are, after all, here to improve their English. Er … good night!' And that was that. Yes, some boys did chat to them, but the fruit no longer forbidden turned out to be not quite as entrancing as had first appeared. At all events, normal life was quickly resumed.

Another occasion did demand Dudley's intervention, although I don't remember what form it took. This was a Labour Party election meeting in the Market Place. Bramston may have had a liberal image in the School, but was solidly Conservative politically. Boys in the studies overlooking the Market Place opened the windows and set up a saucepan-banging, radio-playing diversion designed to disrupt the meeting, in which it succeeded. Was it the October 1951 election, when I was a new boy, or that of May 1955, when I was a senior boy and must be held responsible, even though I am sure I didn't participate? Either way, I remember the event with shame to this day.

Dudley's deputy, the House Tutor, was Sandy Youngman, a suitable choice for Bramston. He was on the music staff, was always jolly and was known as 'Shmoo' apparently because he resembled a pear shaped cartoon character of that name. The House Tutor was always a bachelor – he could hardly be otherwise, since all he had by way of accommodation was a study and a bedroom, and to get from one to the other he had to use the same corridors that led off to the boys' studies. Strange gargling noises sometimes emerged from the Shmoo's study, which, he explained, were his way of practising singing. As a tenor he was always trying to reach ever higher notes. For those of us who were trying to demonstrate our manliness by pitching our voices ever deeper as they broke this seemed a strange and rather dubious endeavour.

Mr Youngman was instrumental in getting Bramston to win the Music Cup shortly after I arrived. The competition was deliberately weighted against Houses that might be tempted to field an ensemble of just one or two excellent musicians. Each House 'orchestra' scored half a point for each player. Mr Youngman exploited this system by arranging a piece for an outsize Bramston orchestra with parts appropriate to each player's abilities, however meagre. I was there, playing my flute after only two or three weeks' tuition, together with an array of percussionists, some of whom couldn't even read music. So Bramston had built up a commanding lead even before we had played a note and duly won: a triumph of House Spirit in which I was a proud participant.

In due course Mr Youngman was replaced by I. D. F. (Ian) Coutts, who generated great excitement as he was a sportsman – an Oxford cricket and rugby Blue and Scottish rugby Cap. It was something of a disappointment that he turned out to be rather a shy and uninspiring geography teacher, who was said to have started a lesson by asserting, 'The Pyrenees are divided into three halves.' Strange music emanated from his room, too, which turned out to be the flute. I was disconcerted to learn that he was taking lessons from my teacher, Bandy Lawes. Masters, in my view, were there to teach, not learn, and I was even more disconcerted when he rather hesitantly asked my advice on some points of technique.

Next in the staff hierarchy came Matron – the prim Miss Emmerson when I arrived and later the more expansive Mrs Brooke-Taylor (mother of Tim Brooke-Taylor, the TV personality and star of *The Goodies*). She afforded me and a couple of other boys one of the two car rides I enjoyed during my whole stay at Oundle – to a nearby school to support our Rugby team. Riding in a car was exciting for me (much more so than the rugby match) and slightly nerve-wracking as we wound our way homewards in the gloom after the match. 'Dusk is always the most dangerous time on the roads,' said Mrs Brooke-Taylor ominously as she sped round the bends, an observation that has remained with me ever since. The force behind these ladies of gentle birth, however, was the down-to-earth Miss Riseborough (Rising Fart, as we rudely called her), who dealt with all our laundry and endless patching and sewing of name tapes for boys whose parents had failed in this duty.

******

Every day we had to leave the cosy confines of our Bramston home to become smaller fish in the larger pool of Oundle School. In the south of England Oundle was not a well known public school. People (especially in railway ticket offices) tended to mishear the name as Arundel. And letters had to be addressed in block capitals, otherwise they would end up in Dundee. But I was grateful that Oundle was not called the Grocers' School after the Livery Company that governed it (compare Haberdashers Askes and the Licensed Victuallers' School). I found it degrading enough to learn that what I had taken to be the nine daggers or swords embellishing the Oundle coat of arms were in fact cloves.

Oundle was solidly patronised by Midlands industrialists and sundry entrepreneurs – Crittall of Crittall's Windows, Cussons of Cussons' soap, Elliman of Elliman's Athletic Rub, Kunzle of Kunzle's Cakes, Owen of Rubery Owen, the big Midlands car dealership of those years (whose father was alleged to have pulled Mum's hair in their youth), the Wontner brothers, whose father owned the Savoy, and Joseph, whose father owned most of the other London hotels. But we in Bramston could boast of having the son of a professor of English at Cambridge, J. I. M. Stewart, who also wrote detective novels under the pen name of Michael Innes, which of course made him exciting as well as prestigious. And one of the famous First World War poets, Siegfried Sassoon, had his son George in New House.

Oundle had a history stretching back far enough for it to be able to celebrate its four hundredth anniversary in 1956, but the school known to Dad and to us boys took wing only at the beginning of the 20th century, when at a low ebb (just ninety two pupils) the Governors put it in the hands of Frederick William Sanderson (1857-1922). He was a man of vision, championed by H. G. Wells (who sent two sons to Oundle and wrote a biography of Sanderson). I had only the haziest idea of what Sanderson's vision was, but knew that it had something to do with the teaching of engineering and applied science and that one of its practical embodiments was the School workshops. This complex of buildings housed a complete manufacturing cycle: a carpentry and pattern-making shop, where you could make a wooden item or a wooden pattern for the foundry, where you would cast your pattern in the appropriate metal; and finally the metal-working shop, where you would finish on lathes what you had cast and make various accessories, such as screws and axles. We all had to do a week in the workshops every term. It was fashionable for my fellow pupils on the arts side to groan about the workshops week, but I loved it, partly because I enjoyed doing things with my hands and partly because it brought me into closer touch with my science and engineering family. I cast a brass dog, but my proudest achievement was a carpenter's marking gauge, which involved making a wooden block in the pattern shop, casting it in aluminium, then boring holes in it (one of them threaded) on metal-working lathes, fashioning a shaft with a sharp disc on the end for marking, and finally making a threaded brass screw to hold the shaft in place. I proudly gave the finished product to Dad, and it found its way into his tool box alongside Robin's rather more expert version made some three years' previously.

The rest of the school schedule was more orthodox. The Oundle timetable is dimmer in my memory than the Forres one, probably because it changed quite substantially as we moved into senior forms and increasingly devised our own timetables with our form masters. We started the day with prayers, alternating between the Great Hall, which dominated the cluster of School buildings in the centre of town, and the Chapel some way out opposite St Anthony House. When prayers were in the Chapel they might be followed by a brief ceremony to award School Colours for sporting achievement. We would all line the Chapel lawn while the relevant School Captain would place himself in the middle and announce a name. The boy so honoured would stride across the lawn, carefully blending pride and modesty, to receive his certificate, on the basis of which he could wear an appropriately coloured scarf and walk around with the collar of his blazer turned up. This apparently trivial sartorial concession was important: it was the way blazers were worn by real sportsmen. I stood at the edge of the lawn dreaming of the day when my turn would come, but of course it never did. At least I was saved the traditional counter-ceremony under which, if he was a Bramstonian, the newly honoured boy would be brought down a peg or two by being unceremoniously debagged on the House lawn before lunch, his trousers ending up as high as possible in the trees down the side of the lawn.

Prayers in the Great Hall were more welcome to me: it was nearer to Bramston, and my form room was in the same building. For all my enthusiasm for the workshops, the School had correctly assessed that science and engineering were not my natural bent, and I was put into Form VA1 for my first year. This was the highest classics/languages form to which new boys could be admitted, and the form master was a suitably august figure, W. G. (Willy) Walker. Like a number of other masters, he had been there in Dad's time. Willy Walker was a dry old stick, but sufficiently good at teaching Latin to enable me to get a formal certificate from the Oxford and Cambridge Schools Examinations Board certifying that I had *satisfied the examiners in Latin taken early for Responsions and the Previous Examination in July 1952.* This mystifying formula (known to us as 'early Latin') meant that I had the necessary Latin qualification for entry to Cambridge and could now give it up, which I did.

Willy Walker also taught us Divinity, analysing in a highly academic way one of the books of the Old Testament to show that it was actually two narratives stitched together. This could have been interesting, but I never got on to his wavelength, so scandalised was I by his deconstructing what I had always been told was a sacred text and moreover getting us to deface our Bibles with red and blue underlining to highlight the different narratives. Perhaps as a reaction to the intellectual rigour of his lessons the class became very adolescent in the breaks, with much horseplay and debagging. I was not much of a one for this and stood primly on the sidelines, a curious observer.

The masters stuck to their own classrooms, so at the end of each lesson we boys scuttled round finding our new room, which could be several minutes' walk away. Most of my classrooms were in the Cloisters. Here on the ground floor Dudley had his room, as did Mr Venning, a kind and gentle man who taught me all the maths I know. Mr Curtis had his room here. He taught me English one year. We paid little attention to his lessons, however, as we knew that at some point he would talk to the class about his experiences in a Japanese prisoner of war camp, which were exciting and repugnant at the same time. He was particularly eloquent on the gradual brutalisation of young guards who had arrived at the camp more or less straight from school. In another ground floor Cloisters class room I was taught English by Rolf Barber, with his RAF moustache. Under his guidance I failed English Literature in my School Certificate – I hadn't understood that one needed not only to know one's materials but to demonstrate this with ample references and quotations. I retook it and passed, by this time knowing the set book, *Twelfth Night*, inside out, having seen it performed professionally and acted in it myself at School.

On the first floor of the Cloisters were two French masters, Hugo Caudwell and Dr B. B. 'Bobby' Rafter. Mr Caudwell, like Dudley Heesom, was a scholar who, it was said, had actually turned down a university lectureship in order to teach at Oundle. He had published a book, *The Creative Impulse*, and had a wide range of interests, including stained glass windows. A rather austere and serious man, he could be pretty withering when he chose. He once returned an essay to the wretched Swallow (the boy who had been marooned with me on Peterborough station) with the words, 'I've given you one mark for pen and one for paper, and nothing for content.' He left me with one pearl of knowledge – that great writers were usually flawed and were open to criticism, even from schoolboys like us. He liked to quote André Gide, who, when asked who he considered to be the greatest French writer, is reported to have said, *'Victor Hugo, hélas !'*

Bobby Rafter was a perfect foil. A large and jovial man with an India rubber face that he could stretch into every conceivable shape, he drilled us, exaggerating wildly, in two phrases with which we could master all French pronunciation. For the nasals it was *Un grand bassin rond;* for the difficult 'u' sound it was *Il y a huit huîtres dans la cuisine.* 'Form your mouth to say "oo", then try to say "ee". All together now: *huit huuiitres dans la cuuuuiiisine.* That's better!' Bobby Rafter had many languages under his belt and towards the end of my time he launched into Russian, informally teaching a couple of volunteers (John Corps and me) while keeping one lesson ahead himself. I had by that time reconciled myself to the idea of teachers learning themselves, and his enthusiasm was to have a profound effect on my life.

Towards the end of my time an attic space in the Cloisters was transformed into a Modern Languages Library. I used it ever more frequently as a quiet reading room during free periods or to get away from my study in Bramston, which with some half dozen occupants was rarely quiet. The Modern Languages Library was much more to my taste than the gloomy School Library in the Great Hall. Here I was captivated by books I had picked up at random – Alain-Fournier's romantic novel of schoolboy love *Le Grand Meaulnes* and Hugh Thomas's history of the Spanish Civil War. The latter was a real eye opener to one reared on the heroic, good versus bad books and films of the Second World War: it showed a war that had been exceedingly cruel and where both sides were bad.

My most eccentric French teacher (and form master for my year in the Modern [languages] Remove, one step up from VA1) had his classroom outside the Cloisters in a side street off the Market Place, one of the many odd buildings the School had acquired over the years to cope with its growth. He was C. A. B. 'Cabby' Marshall. He was gay – not that we used that term or cared particularly about his sexuality. He had a delightful disregard for the accepted norms of healthy life (he resolutely refused to open the windows of his classroom, saying 'Fresh air is for – *outside!*') or for conventional wisdom ('Funerals are *so* much more fun than weddings.'). We knew that as Arthur Marshall he was already quite a name in the broadcasting world (he wrote and starred in a wartime BBC radio comedy series, *A Date with Nurse Dugdale*), but what mattered was that he brought his sense of fun into the classroom. He even made learning vocabulary fun (*Bouillabaisse*: fish soup – *with garlic!*). He was quite a hard task master, arguing convincingly that a score of fifty or sixty per cent in your vocabulary test was not good enough – it would still leave you tongue-tied in real life. But he made the tests fun by instituting a finely graded series of prizes (tokens for the School bookshop and paid for, no doubt, out of his own pocket). I won a *Petit Prix de Mémoire (Première Classe)* and with my token bought a book called *Simple Heraldry, Cheerfully Illustrated.* 'What a *jolly* book,' said Cabby, approvingly.

Cabby's unique contribution to Oundle was his occasional production of *Masterpieces*, an end-of-term revue starring most of the staff. There's nothing boys (and others) like more than seeing their mentors make fools of themselves, as long as it's done well, and with Cabby at the helm it was. Cabby of course featured in one of his favourite roles as a jolly-hockey-sticks schoolgirl, but what remains in my memory was a brief, wordless sketch in which he appeared as a mourning Queen Victoria, motionless in a wicker chair, eyes fixed on the horizon, while an off-stage piano intoned 'Land of Hope and Glory'. Imperceptibly, the music took on the theme of 'Oh, I do love to be beside the seaside!' After an agonising period (a couple of seconds, perhaps) when we, the audience, had realised what was happening and 'Queen Victoria' hadn't, she jerked her head up, the music instantaneously changed back to the original theme and the Queen subsided again.

Cabby could be peevish at times, without any apparent reason. It was fairly obvious that, like many masters of comedy, he was rather a sad and lonely man underneath the jollity. But we saw it as something of a betrayal when he suddenly upped and left to become secretary (*secretary* – wasn't that a low status job done by women?) to Viscount Rothschild, the eminent zoologist and public figure, in Cambridge. Later on Cabby returned to the public eye in a more appropriate role on the TV show *Call My Bluff*.

While my French teachers were higher quality, it was to Spanish that I was drawn. It was, after all, a familiar language in our family. Outside Latin and French there was a choice of languages, and I was originally assigned to do ancient Greek. I was dead against Greek, probably because I had never mastered the basics in the way the other boys seemed to have done, so I wrote to Dad asking if I could change to Spanish (I must have been too awe-struck by the masters to approach them direct). Dad wrote to Dudley, and the matter was soon settled. Our Spanish set was taught in a small classroom in an old building off the Cloisters by another eccentric, 'Tub' Shaw. Small and rotund, as his nick-name implied, he allowed us to address him to his face as 'Tub' and never stood on his dignity, standing on a table instead if he felt the need to assert his authority. The first book we read was *Platero y Yo*, by Juan Ramón Jiménez, a whimsical set of prose poems about a donkey in Andalucía that I alternately loved and hated, depending on my mood.

In my Spanish set I sat next to the only Thai boy in the School at the time. Oundle had a long history of hosting Thai students. To have been educated at a British public school was something of a prize, and in earlier days some of the Thai students had been rather more mature than they made themselves out to be, their Oriental appearance successfully masking their age. Dad enjoyed telling the story of one in his day who lost his temper with an officious master: 'You can't talk to me like that – I'm a married man with children!' he blurted out, before being sent packing to rejoin his family. My exotic class mate, M. R. Tongnoi Tongyai ('Tong' to all), was genuinely my age and a good friend, who taught me how to write my name in Siamese, but the fact that we were in different Houses (he was in St Anthony, of course) meant that we were never that close. In all my time at Oundle I never once set foot in another House, and I don't remember any boy from another House coming to Bramston. Tong spent most of his career on the staff of the King of Thailand.

My other Spanish teacher was A. G. 'Flossy' Payne, for whom I had little liking. From the start I had a prejudice against him because his academic hood, unlike those of all the other masters I could think of, did not sport the red of Oxford or white of Cambridge, but the muddy hue of some 'second class' university. He had a steely eye and distant manner, maybe on account of having been an interrogator during the war, as I learnt many years later. He found me hard going, too. 'He refuses to be exciting,' he wrote in one report.

It was up to the boys or their parents to organise practical language training by visits to France, Spain or Germany. My first trip to Spain was in April 1955. I was fortunate to have a welcoming home in Madrid: 'Hendy' Henderson and his wife Jo had been Shell friends of Mum and Dad in Argentina – Hendy became Jonathan's godfather – and now they were posted in Madrid. Hospitable and generous to a fault, they even found me a local medical student, Manolo, quite a few years older than me, to shepherd me around Madrid and chat in Spanish, which he did with a will. They must have rewarded him somehow; otherwise I can't imagine what would have induced him to give up so much time to this awkward teenager. One day he took me to watch an operation in his medical school, which put me off my food for the rest of the day. It was not so much the operation itself that shocked me as the way the staff roughly pulled the patient out of his anaesthetised state, slapping him on the face and shouting '¡*Abre los ojos!*' ('Open your eyes!') Manolo also 'introduced' me to his fiancée, which involved waving to her as she sat with her mother on the balcony of her tenement block. Under the strict social code still in force in Spain, that was about as close as he would get to her until they were safely married. It didn't worry Manolo, as under the same code it was tacitly accepted that he could meanwhile involve himself in whatever amorous adventures he pleased. My trip to France in September of the same year with Mavis was intended to put my spoken French to the test, which it did. Despite Cabby Marshall's vocabulary tests I was seized with panic at having to use French 'live' after a decade of academic study and couldn't even find the French for 'potato'.

Science took up only a small part of my timetable. In my first year our form would visit the Science Block, up the road from the Great Hall, for Biology, and I see from my reports that I did quite well in the subject. I never took to it, however. The master, Mr Coulson, was dull, but more important was that I never learnt to use a microscope properly. Boys wearing spectacles were still a rarity, and I never knew whether to look through the instrument with my glasses on or off. I was reduced to drawing what I thought I ought to

Off to France: with Mavis in front of
Warwick Lodge, August 1955

be seeing rather than what I was seeing, which was a blur, most of the time. In the following year we had a more exciting time in the Science Block. This was a weekly general science class with H. C. 'Bungy' Palmer, every bit the 'mad' scientist – rotund, unkempt and so short-sighted that he brought instruments to within millimetres of his eyes. His concern was to get us to understand that science was not a cerebral pursuit, but something done by practically-minded, intensely curious people in the kitchen, in the fields, or up a mountain. So he was disappointed (as he confessed to Robin, not to us) when in the fairly light-hearted exam he set us at the end of our first term one boy started his description of an experiment, 'Take two mountains ...' It wasn't me, I'm glad to say, and I came first in the class in that exam, but my flame seems to have burnt low after that and I only got 'satisfactory' on my next report. So, in this most scientific of schools my science education finished before I was sixteen, and I focused ever more narrowly on French and Spanish. When I reached the Sixth Form – Modern VIC, Modern VIB and finally Modern VIA, I was providing employment for two Spanish and two French teachers simultaneously. By today's GCSE standards the range of subjects I took for 'O' Levels in the summer of 1953 was narrow: English Language and Literature; French; Spanish; Elementary Maths; and Additional Maths. In 1954 I took just two 'A' Levels, French and Spanish.

Art and music were also on the academic curriculum, that is to say they figured in my reports, but without the burden of exams. Art was always enjoyable and for me it was unexpectedly useful. In the 1950s the revival of the Elizabethan or Italic style of handwriting reached schools – initially as an art form. In art class we did our own 'illuminated manuscripts'. Then I tried the style for ordinary handwriting and found that the special thick nib that I used imposed a new discipline on the way I formed letters. I was encouraged by the masters, some of whom had taken up this style as well, and was commended for 'Good work, most attractively written' by Mr Caudwell, an amazing reversal of my dismal record at Forres. I then took up oil painting and was rewarded by winning the School Landscape Prize. I was embarrassed at this because the boy everyone expected to win could reproduce landscapes with photographic accuracy while my work was a series of crude blobs. This was of course exactly what the judges were looking for – a painterly naivety. Oil painting became one of the principal hobbies of my late teens and early twenties. The pleasant and relaxed art master for most of my time was Mr Mackenzie, who, like Mrs Brooke-Taylor, induced panic by his driving. On the second and final occasion I rode in a car at Oundle we were coming back from an art exhibition in Peterborough in pitch darkness with the headlights of Mr Mackenzie's ancient Rolls pointing anywhere but on the road ahead. 'I … I don't think your headlights are properly adjusted, sir,' I ventured to say. 'I know,' he replied airily, 'but they make *such* a lovely pattern on the trees.'

My musical career was more complex, although it seemed simple at the time. I arrived as an indifferent pianist and continued thus for my first term under the kindly but uninspiring guidance of Mr Edmonds, a cellist, who in turn found that my playing 'seldom appears spontaneous'. The idea was then mooted that I should take up an orchestral instrument, as many boys did, and in discussion with Dad we opted for the flute on a number of purely practical grounds – relatively cheap, no troublesome reeds and, above all, not too jarring on the ear when played by a beginner. Mr Edmonds had assumed that I was taking up the flute in addition to the piano, and on hearing that it was instead of said, 'You'll regret that.' I do.

There was a dedicated Music School just off the main road, halfway between Bramston and New House. All the woodwind and brass instruments were taught by just one man, ex-Bandmaster G. A. 'Bandy' Lawes, who had trained at The Royal Military School of Music, Kneller Hall, in Twickenham and had once lived in Amyand Park Road, near to our own St Margaret's station. Bandy Lawes was a genial and blunt character who liked to call his pupils 'professor'. Jack of all trades (he also played the cello) but master of only one, the bassoon, Bandy taught me all sorts of tricks to get round awkward corners, including some wrong fingering, as I learnt many years later. Like my piano teachers, he presented me with some rather too sophisticated pieces for a beginner. I still take out and work on the copy of Bach's *Sonata in A minor* he presented to me, with his initials in the corner – one of the most exacting pieces in the repertoire, but an obvious choice for beginners in those days simply because it covered only a limited range of the modern flute.

After a couple of terms it was judged that I should have a flute of my own, so at some point in the holidays in 1952 I nervously presented myself at Rudall Carte, Flute Makers, whose shop was at 23 Berners Street, off Oxford Street. There I met Bandy Lawes' contact, another Kneller Hall veteran, who took one of several second hand cocuswood flutes off the rack and asked me to try it. I blew a few fuzzy notes and pronounced myself satisfied – I could hardly have done otherwise at that stage. The flute was sent to Bandy Lawes for his approval, and shortly after the beginning of term Dad stumped up sixty pounds for it. I have played on no other flute since. In this era of metal flutes mine now attracts an attention it never did earlier, when wooden flutes were all the only ones to be seen.

My first term on the flute coincided with the House Music Competition that I described earlier. Bramston won, and a legend about my ability as a flautist was born. In his Housemaster's report Dudley wrote:

His achievement in playing the flute in the House Orchestra in his first term with the instrument is remarkable.

No musician himself, Dudley probably didn't realise that Sandy Youngman had written me a part exactly suited to my very limited abilities. From that moment on I was assumed to have more talent than I really had, and my weaknesses were carefully concealed (Oundle spurned the Associated Board exams that might have revealed them). I joined the School orchestra and played the very difficult 'bird' part in Prokofiev's *Peter and the Wolf*, cleverly simplified by Bandy Lawes, and I was also given the wonderful flute *obbligato* in the *Domine Deo* from Bach's *Mass in B minor*. But I coped with that only because I had a guardian angel sitting behind me in the shape of Hubert Brand, distinguished amateur flautist,

Oundle contemporary of Dad's and father of Adam Brand, then a precocious little oboe player, now a neighbour and friend. Mr Brand 'shadowed' me, expertly filling in the high notes that I couldn't quite manage. My nemesis came towards the end of my time at Oundle with an instrumental competition, where I came second to last out of some 20 competitors, even below Booth from New House, who was younger than me (and therefore by my definition worse) and played second flute in the orchestra. My only consolation was that the bottom place was occupied by the boy who was probably the most musical of all the competitors – 'Delius' (David in reality) Watkins. He had chosen to play the harp, in which he was self taught, and he had, moreover, made his own instrument in the workshops. Many years later I was delighted to see his unmistakeable figure among the harpists at a concert in Prague given by a visiting London orchestra. He became one of the country's leading harp players and a professor at the Guildhall School of Music.

In music, as elsewhere, I had a great fear of getting out of my depth. Not only had I given up the piano but I resolutely refused to attempt anything with my voice, so until I joined the School orchestra, I was co-opted into that hundreds-strong body known as the 'non-choir' for our annual all-School oratorio performances. These were a major School event, and some well-known soloists took part. Why they came I don't know, as I doubt they were paid much and not much was laid on for them. I remember one bitter disappointment in Handel's *Messiah*, when after some hurried consultation towards the end it was announced that we would be omitting the heart-melting soprano aria *I know that my Redeemer liveth*. The reason? The soprano had to get home that night and feared missing the last train back. On another occasion the tenor William McAlpine was billeted on Bramston, and after the concert Dudley took it into his head to take him around the freezing dormitory and introduce him to all the boys, already tucked up in bed. 'This is Nicholson, he plays the flute,' and so on, methodically, totally unaware that the wretched McAlpine was pulling his scarf ever more tightly around his throat, desperately afraid of catching the cold that would put paid to his next few engagements. Next morning we were agog to see what he made of our breakfast as he took his seat opposite Dudley in the centre of the dining room. 'Er … I'm afraid I don't eat porridge,' he admitted nervously, and then, 'I don't eat bacon either!' on being presented with a limp and fatty rasher on a thick slice of fried bread. After that ordeal I was always relieved to see and hear William McAlpine in good voice on the opera and oratorio circuit.

We also had some big names at the series of Sunday afternoon subscription concerts that Dad generously paid for us boys to attend, among them Benjamin Britten and Peter Pears, and Gerald Moore, the man who put accompanists on the map, with his book *Am I Too Loud?* I was captivated by the informality and sheer humanity that most of these famous people radiated. One well-known lady pianist put at ease an unfortunate boy in the front row wracked by a fit of coughing. Between movements she dipped into her handbag and with the sweetest of smiles tossed a cough lozenge straight into his lap before moving imperturbably into the next movement.

I always auditioned for the School play, but the best I achieved was a 'bit' part in *Twelfth Night*. I was very disappointed to be cast as an ancient priest with just eight lines to speak. Having heard me reciting them mechanically and somewhat sulkily the producer, Mr Burns, tactfully suggested that I should look into this character more closely – why does he take eight lines to answer the simple question of whether he has just married the young couple before him? This was the tip I needed, and I turned the Priest into an indefatigable rambler and bore, to great acclaim. On the strength of this, in my last summer term after exams Mr Curtis offered me the substantial part of the Prior in Dorothy L. Sayers' *The Zeal of Thy House*, a religious drama based on an incident that occurred during the burning and rebuilding of the choir at Canterbury Cathedral in the 12th century. Mr Curtis had adapted it for the Oundle Parish Church. Throwing aside fears of becoming type-cast I jumped at the opportunity and enjoyed it, apart from having to parade in monk's garb in the School Cloisters during our rehearsals. Good publicity, said Mr C.

We all knew, however, that sport rather than academic or artistic achievement was the real measure of the worth of the individual, the House and the School. Whether your House rugby team came back victorious with arms linked, taking up the road and singing, or whether they trudged home singly or in dispirited groups, determined the House Spirit over the coming weeks if not months. Graham Stainforth, the Headmaster, once called the whole School together to contrast the School rowing Eight's performance at Henley (uplifting) with the behaviour of one quite mature boy caught snogging a skivvy behind the swimming baths (repulsive).

It was of course my dream to be part of a victorious team, be it rugby or cricket, and I tried my best, including taking some cricket coaching classes at Lord's (paid for by Dad no doubt), to no avail. I just wasn't talented enough at ball games, and rowing was not for one as small as I – though like most boys I took the 'boat test', which involved being thrown into the river Nene in full rugby kit and swimming to the bank. The one sport for which I did have some natural talent, thanks to my slow heart rate, was athletics, which we did towards the end of the Lent Term. The early- to mid-fifties was the era of the great British middle-distances runners – Bannister, Chataway (an Old Forresian and therefore a particular favourite), Brasher and Derek Johnson, who once came down to Oundle to give us an afternoon's coaching. I followed their fortunes in minute detail and dreamt of emulating them. Athletics, not being a 'team' sport, occupied a lower rung than rugby, cricket or rowing in the Oundle scale of prestige sports, but there was a cup to be won by the House with the best aggregate score over several days of competition. When Robin was House athletics captain he took a leaf out of Sandy Youngman's book, figuring out that since athletic talent was spread fairly thinly through the School, Bramston might pick up the odd third place in the more obscure events simply by saturating the whole competition with its own athletes, however indifferent their performance. Accordingly, he put all our names down for every event, which didn't win him much popularity in the House and for me led to a rare moment of annoyance with my otherwise impeccable elder brother, especially when I landed in a humiliating heap after a vain attempt at a pole vault. I don't think we won the cup, either.

Separately, there was a School cross country race and a competition for the Mile. In Bramston we had an enthusiastic leader for these events in Piers Recordon, a wise and humane fellow and good clarinettist a year or so older than me, with whom I had many earnest conversations at School and later at House dinners, when he had become a GP in Cambridge. He was a doctor's son and took advice from his father on diet (spinach and boiled eggs on the day of the event, which we prepared ourselves, ignoring the official House lunch). When I became House athletics captain I tried to emulate Piers by instilling Team Spirit into the House cross country runners. I would take a group of enthusiasts out for a training run after the compulsory sport for the day was over. They were a motley crew.

Athletes: In 1952 Bramston won the Gale Cup for the Mile
under the Captaincy of Piers Recordon (centre). I am on the right,
in front of Dudley Heesom

A number were completely inept at ball games and too weedy to row, so for years had been sent on local runs while the rest of the House had done its team sports. Thanks to this endless enforced training some of them had become quite strong runners. But on the day I ran for myself, like everyone else. I came twelfth, not bad, but not good enough to earn those coveted House colours, or even a place in the School cross country team.

At Forres I had so enjoyed scouting that I immediately joined the Scouts on arrival at Oundle. This was a mistake. I didn't feel at home with the Oundle Scouts, and there was a counter-attraction in the shape of the Combined Cadet Force (CCF). Until shortly before I arrived it had been known at the Officers' Training Corps (OTC) and to us was simply the Corps. I was not militarily minded, but the herd instinct operated, and I knew that at some point every boy had to pass a basic exam in the Corps called Certificate A. So why delay? In the Corps we did drill, map reading, crawling in the undergrowth and shooting. We spent hours maintaining our uniform, particularly applying 'blanco' (a whitening substance) to belts and gaiters, polishing our boots and buffing up our brass cap badges and buckles with Duraglit (Durashit in the vernacular). Happy was the boy who was issued with an old badge that years of polishing had worn smooth. Newer badges, which refused to shine because of their high relief, would be surreptitiously taken to the workshops for a serious application of abrasive. And new berets, which made the wearer look like a French onion seller, would be forcibly 'aged' until they looked more soldierly.

A number of masters doubled as CCF officers, but its backbone was provided by one man, Captain R. M. Lacey, an ex-Marine, small, dapper, impeccably turned out and totally dedicated. Away from the parade ground we made fun of him and his single mindedness (boys to him were 'cadets', whatever they were doing), but we did his bidding pretty smartly when under his orders, not a bad state of affairs when we were carrying loaded rifles on the shooting range. The highlight of the Corps programme was Field Day. We rushed around, executing incomprehensible manoeuvres that would leave swathes of us 'dead' without our knowing why, but our main concern was simply to keep at bay the raging discomfort caused by our thick serge uniforms in the summer heat. The answer was to wear pyjamas next to the skin. Although they added an extra layer at least they absorbed the itching. One Field Day I found myself separated from my squad, all alone in a field, shielded from the sun by a huge oak tree, contemplating the cows in the distance while flies hovered over the cowpats. Unlikely as it seems, and despite the heat, I experienced a sense of total peace that for years afterwards I was able to recreate at will to calm myself down or induce sleep.

When I had passed 'Cert A' I had had enough of real 'soldiering' and joined the Corps band. We paraded at the Music School under the command of 'Bandy' Reed. He was a bandsman rather than Bandmaster, and his jaw muscles were so developed from years of playing the horn that his face had assumed the shape of a pyramid. Acutely conscious of his modest educational level he tended to overcompensate with his language: he would never begin at the beginning, but always 'commence at the commencement'. He was also modest about his musical skills, and it was with extreme embarrassment that he once shyly presented us with a piece he had written himself. I liked it, as it was playable, and I can still remember the simple tune of the trio section. We played from music he had meticulously copied by hand on to postcard-size cards, which were attached to instruments (or in the case of the flute to the forearm) with special clips, so that we could play on the march.

The flute wasn't much of an instrument to play in the open air, the soft sound being quickly borne away on the wind. Indeed on some days the wind would whip away the air stream from the mouth before it even reached the embouchure of the flute, so no sound came out at all. No matter, I could scarcely play my parts anyway, since they were difficult to read, right up at the top of the instrument, many tiny ledger lines above the stave, and were moreover usually a complex elaboration over the top of some sturdy tune being blared out by the clarinets and trumpets. The upstart Booth cleverly took up the piccolo, which was a much more effective band instrument. It took me longer to learn that the piccolo was a useful adjunct to the flute.

******

As my time at School neared its end University and National Service loomed. University meant St Catharine's College, Cambridge, where Dad had been and Robin was. No other option was considered. On 17th November 1954 I went for an admission interview with Tom Henn, the Senior Tutor, and an expert on W. B. Yeats. He sat me down in a deep sofa, and his large retriever immediately jumped on top of me, so I spent the entire interview half buried in cushions and dog. Tom Henn was a kindly soul, who knew Dad and Robin and was only marginally disappointed at my evident lack of achievement on the rugby field. Only one of his questions floored me: 'How do you intend to finance yourself?' Finance *myself*? I thought that was something parents did. I mumbled that I hoped to get a scholarship, then weakly admitted that my father would finance me, which he probably knew all along.

A few days later Dudley mentioned in passing that Cath's wanted to have me. In agonies of doubt I sought reassurance that I was really in, after such a cursory interview, so Dudley showed me the letter he had received from Tom Henn:

Dear Mr Heesom

We interviewed your pupil M.B.Nicholson at some length yesterday. He is obviously an acceptable person on academic grounds as well as for family reasons, and we are prepared to confirm his admission for 1957. We are not quite clear whether you think it would be to his advantage to sit for the Scholarship Examination in February/March in the hope of getting into the Exhibition class, or to concentrate on the G.C.E. at "S" level in the hope of getting a State. But I think these decisions had best be left to you.

I am writing separately to Nicholson's father.

What he wrote to Dad was:

My dear Nicholson

We saw your boy yesterday and liked him well. I enclose a copy of a letter that I have written to his Housemaster, which I think explains matters.

I was at a Kittens dinner last night with his brother, who seems to be developing extremely well and is a balanced and mature person.

And that was that. I didn't try for the St Catharine's scholarship. I did the same two 'A' levels again in the hope of raising my marks to the 'S', or scholarship, level, but didn't achieve that. Nonetheless I was awarded a means tested Major County Award from Middlesex County Council, which helped Dad pay for my tuition fees. Tom Henn's letter had envisaged me coming up to Cath's in October 1957, which would have meant leaving Oundle in July 1955, just before my eighteenth birthday, so as to do my National Service as soon as I was 18. In the event I stayed on for the Michaelmas Term and left only at Christmas, thus setting everything back one year. I don't remember why this was: the most likely explanation being that I had been told I wouldn't be called up till the following year.

I had a pleasant Summer Term after the exams and then a pleasant Michaelmas Term with nothing particular to do. By this time I was not only a House prefect, No 2 under Gobby Clark, but also a School prefect. Together with another boy I had been invited to lunch by the Headmaster, who gave us a glass of sherry and was generally affable. We knew this meant we were in line for School prefectship (Heads of House were School prefects *ex officio* plus two or three others) and in due course this honour came our way. 'I hope you do something with it, unlike your brother,' said Christopher Morgan sternly. I bridled a bit at the slight on Robin and I'm sure I disappointed Morgan, since I did nothing as a School prefect beyond enjoying the status (self-importantly processing into Great Hall and Chapel, and wearing a distinctive tie in contrast to the standard black) and privileges (a School prefects' Common Room in the Cloisters and the right to shop where and when we liked).

******

I had already laid my plans for National Service, one of the two constant topics of discussion among us leavers. (The other was the driving test, of no interest to me, since the family was still car-less.) Here two strands came together that were to determine my professional life. I have mentioned that Bobby Rafter started teaching me Russian. I had long been fascinated by the strange alphabet and wanted to be able to write the name of my favourite Russian composer, Tchaikovsky, in it. I was delighted to find that the awkward first three consonants in the English spelling were formed by a single consonant in Russian. I was a little disconcerted to find that the final 'y' was represented by one and a half vowels in Russian, then positively discouraged by learning that this was only in the *nominative* case, and that his name went all over the place in the other cases. Shades of Latin and Greek! I was on the point of giving up when I learnt of the possibility of learning Russian in National Service. The Services needed to train staff who knew the language of the potential enemy – this was at the height of the Cold War – and national servicemen, who could be recalled in an emergency, were the ideal material.

We gleaned this intelligence from a visiting Old Oundelian who had either done the course himself or knew someone who had. We also learnt that the Navy was the best service to join. In the Navy you would be ear-marked for the Russian course from the moment you joined up, whereas in the other two services you could only apply after your basic training, and might meet with total incomprehension from your camp commander. So I took steps to join the Royal Naval Volunteer Reserve (RNVR) and thus ensure I was effectively in the Navy before my call-up came. I nearly came unstuck at my interview in Cambridge (not at Cath's this time but a dingy barracks), because I had no knowledge of intelligence tests and little of the Navy. But the kindly supervising Petty Officer whispered some of the answers and I got in.

I was officially accepted into the RNVR in August 1954, just after my seventeenth birthday. My poor eyesight meant that I couldn't be taken on as a seaman, and although it was understood that I would do the Russian course when I joined the Navy proper there was no provision for it in the RNVR, so I signed on as a Junior Stores Assistant (Victualling). Happily, I never had to find out what this meant in practice. In the summer of 1955 I did a fortnight of basic training in the aircraft carrier HMS *Theseus*, refitted as a training ship and safely tied up in Portland Harbour. There I learnt how to sling a hammock and sleep in it and how to distinguish between coffee and tea (the first was served in the morning and the second in the afternoon, both so heavily diluted with condensed milk as to suppress any other taste, and both – according to the wags – also laced with bromide to suppress the sexual urge). My companions were public school types, who went drinking in Weymouth every evening while I, ever the swot, stayed on board studying manuals, as a result of which I came first in our end-of-course exam, to general surprise. My only venture ashore was on our free Sunday, when I hitch-hiked to Swanage and surprised Mr & Mrs Chadwick having tea in the garden. I must have been a curious sight in my brand new, thick serge fore-and-aft uniform (i.e. with collar and tie, as worn by clerical grades, not the real sailors' 'square rig'), but they made me feel at home.

At the end of term the Headmaster gave us leavers a pep-talk in the library and warned against sex ('Don't think you're not a man till you've had a woman') and alcohol ('Beware of the short drink habit'). The first seemed sensible enough, but the second puzzled me, since I didn't know what a short drink was. When I found out I was even more puzzled. Wasn't it Mr Stainforth himself who had introduced me to the short drink habit with that glass of sherry at lunch? And were Mum and Dad on the road to ruin now that they had begun to allow themselves the occasional drink before a meal? I think he had in mind that most of us would be going straight into the Forces and a number would end up in the Officers' Mess, where the path to the dinner table always went past the bar.

At all events, having arrived at Oundle aware of the perils of crossing invisible lines, I left four and a half years later facing the temptations of sex and alcohol. I was not yet an adult, but my childhood was definitely over.

23052040R00106

Printed in Great Britain
by Amazon